Mapping Trophy Bucks

Using Topographic Maps to Find Deer

Brad Herndon

Published by

krause publications
An Imprint of F+W Publications

700 East State Street • Iola, WI 54990-0001
715-445-2214 • 888-457-2873
www.krausebooks.com

Our toll-free number to place an order or obtain a free catalog is (800) 258-0929.

Library of Congress Catalog Number: 2003108888
ISBN 13-digit: 978-0-87349-503-5
ISBN 10-digit: 0-87349-503-9

Printed in the United States of America

Edited by Kevin Michalowski
Designed by Jon Stein and Tom Nelsen

Acknowledgments

Brad and Carol Herndon.

Many people have contributed to the success I have been privileged to enjoy in the outdoor field. Back in 1986 Leonard Lee Rue III suggested I take up writing along with my outdoor photography. Although he doesn't realize it, he was directly responsible for me becoming an author. Local author Carl Wells edited my first few stories and gave me valuable guidance. In 1987 Gordon Whittington of *North American Whitetail* magazine bought the first article I wrote: The Making Of A Trophy Hunter. Al Hofacker of *Deer & Deer Hunting* magazine published my work shortly thereafter.

Many others involved with *Deer & Deer Hunting* magazine and Krause Publications, past and present, also get a pat on the back. Don Gulbrandsen, Pat Durkin, Dan Schmidt and Brian Lovett all have been great to work with. And certainly I needed an excellent editor like Kevin Michalowski to keep my southern Indiana grammar readable for hunters in other parts of North America.

And I'm deeply grateful to Gerry Bethge of Harris Publications for allowing me to curtail my writing schedule for him so I could write this book for Krause Publications. Not many magazine editors would have been so understanding and thoughtful.

I also want to thank Bill Jordan, David Blanton, and many others at Realtree Camouflage who have treated my wife Carol and I like family for so many years. Bill Jordan gave us the opportunity and time to develop our photography skills. And much of what we know about photography we owe to the fair and gentle guidance of Dodd Clifton.

I owe my love of nature to my father and mother, Paul and Doris Herndon, and to my grandmother Freda "Nanny" Leffler. All are gone now, but not forgotten. They gave me a well-rounded background in hunting, fishing, berry-picking, mushroom hunting, tree, flower and insect identification, and various other outdoor hobbies.

On the deer hunting side, Jay Mellencamp introduced me to my first topographical map back in the 1970s. A master strategist perhaps 20 years ahead of his time, his knowledge and room full of trophy whitetails inspired me to explore the mysterious world of the mature whitetail buck. Cullen Stahl, "The Midday Master," proved to me big bucks could be taken consistently during midday. Howard A. "Bud" Osborne has been a terrific inspiration to me as he suffered numerous serious illnesses and still hangs tough as a deer hunter. Zen "The Kentuckian" Caudill proved time and time again that there was no deer too big for an old blackpowder gun.

A lot of credit goes to my younger deer hunting friends, too. Henry Reynolds, Anthony Moore, Junior Stuckwisch, Spencer Williams, and numerous other local hunters have served as willing models for many of the deer hunting photographs I have taken and sold throughout the years. They keep me young and teach this old dog new hunting tricks from time to time.

Finally I want to thank my wife, Carol, for being a super wife, mother, cook, business partner, and one terrific deer hunter. We enjoyably share our life together every day of the year, with much of our time spent outdoors. No man could have been blessed with a more compatible partner in life than I have been.

And although I have been able to teach her how to become an outstanding whitetail hunter, she has done much more for me. Carol has always had a deep love for the Lord, and has been instrumental in me coming to know Jesus Christ in a much deeper way. If my name gets in "The Book" it will be largely because of her example.

About The Author

Brad Herndon was born and raised in southern Indiana in the pleasant valley of Starve Hollow. Bordered by two ranges of hills with two river bottoms meandering through the region, this outdoor setting allowed Herndon to learn about and appreciate nature to the fullest. He quickly became interested in hunting and fishing. In the 1980s he embarked on an outdoor photography and writing career.

Herndon began hunting deer in 1968 and became fascinated with the way whitetails used terrain. For the past 15 years his articles on deer hunting strategies have been well received by whitetail enthusiasts.

Herndon is currently the hunting editor of *Whitetail Hunting Strategies* magazine, and his work appears in *Outdoor Life, Deer & Deer Hunting*, and numerous other deer hunting magazines. His photography has won several awards from the Outdoor Writers Association of America. The author and his wife, Carol, have taken many of the national ad pictures currently seen in numerous outdoor hunting magazines.

Herndon and his wife live in a cozy log house in the edge of the hills near Brownstown, Indiana. Carol is also an accomplished photographer and works full-time in the family photojournalism business. Carol is also an avid hunter, and as you will see, she kills as many good bucks as the author.

Author Brad Herndon.

Introduction

As I inched along the steep hillside, the faint indentation of a trail turned uphill as it approached a deep gully containing a gurgling stream. The trail paralleled the gully for approximately 100 yards toward the top of the hill, and then turned abruptly to the right, leading me over a rock bluff at the head of the gully. I paused to watch the water cascade over the rocks into the ravine below. Standing in awe, I wondered how many Native Americans had experienced this same feeling at the same waterfall. There was, on top of the hill, an old Indian camp overlooking the bottomland of the White River.

Watching and listening for squirrels, I moved a few feet along the trial and paused. The 8 inches of rain that had fallen over the past two days had washed away many of the leaves, and there in the middle of the trail lay a 4-inch-long flint spear point.

The dark gray projectile had a wider notch on one side of the base than on the other side, identifying it as an Adena point. Here was an artifact several thousand years old and it was proof that hunters in this area pursued big game.

But at the time I found the spear point the region in which I was hunting had virtually no deer. In spite of this, the location of the spear point and the fact that I was there to find it point out that terrain features will cause both wild animals and humans to naturally use the same paths. Fascinatingly, the Native American who dropped the spear point walked the same route I did, even though we lived thousands of years apart.

The geography creates a natural funnel. And now, with whitetails once more abundant in Indiana, the trail near the waterfall is a deathtrap for deer.

The entire point here is that good hunters find the places where terrain works to their advantage. These places will provide the astute whitetail hunter with a crack at a super buck. Although they should be obvious, many of these strategic locations go largely unnoticed.

You will find as you read this book that topographical, aerial and plat maps will enable you to sit at home and pick out great ambush spots, even if your hunting area is hundreds of miles away. Maps may also reveal strategic stand sites, ones you have overlooked, on the land you are presently hunting. This has happened to me more than once. I'll admit I walked through one of my top deer hunting funnels many times over the years before I recognized it for what it was. I noticed the importance of the spot as I was looking at a topographical map one night in my easy chair.

This book will teach you to see a variety of terrain features that influence deer movement. Hilltop field funnels, saddles, converging hubs, and more; all will become familiar terms to you. Then when you recognize one of the hot ambush sites in the woods, you can use the details presented here to figure out how best to hunt the location and allow the terrain to funnel deer to where you will be waiting.

This is the most comprehensive amount of information ever compiled about using topographical and aerial maps while deer hunting. The information is easy to understand and can be mastered by almost any ambitious deer hunter. In the past only the most skillful hunters knew how to use terrain features to their advantage. Now, with modern tools, you can quickly and easily predict how topography can work for you.

Contents

The ability to read topographical maps will enable you to place your tree stands in strategic deer travel corridors, considerably improving your chances of bagging a big buck.

Chapter 1
Tools of the
Terrain Trade

During the early 1980s the Muscatatuck National Wildlife Refuge in Indiana was opened to deer hunting for the first time. The goal was to reduce the rapidly expanding whitetail population within the refuge. Special drawings were held to determine who would have access to this never-before-hunted patch of real estate that contained some awesome bucks. The first hunts were held in December.

One night in mid-November I received a call from Carey Lambring, a good friend of mine.

"Brad, I need some help!" he said excitedly. "I've been drawn for the special muzzleloader hunt in Muscatatuck. Can you help me."

"Sure," I replied. " I have a topographical map of the region. Come down later tonight and we'll see what I can find that will funnel the deer and give you a crack at a dandy buck."

As we pored over the topographical (topo) map, it didn't take long to see several stand sites in the flat terrain. One of the most interesting features, however, was a narrow strip of woods that connected a large tract of timber and a vast swamp.

"Carey," I said as I pointed at the map, "see this big chunk of woods to the east. There should be a lot of deer, and hunters, in this region. Notice how two fairly narrow strips of timber come out of this woods, meander about half way across this open field, then join together to form a very narrow funnel of timber that travels another half mile to a large swamp. When hunters start moving around in the big woods, deer will use this funnel to travel between the two types of cover. If you get some type of north or south wind, you can put your stand in this funnel just west of the "Y" and you should have an excellent opportunity of getting a crack at a good buck."

The next time I saw Lambring was the afternoon of the day he was supposed to hunt the refuge. He pulled up in my driveway, and showed me a dandy 11-point buck in the bed of his truck.

"Your advice worked to perfection," Lambring said. "I had a northeast wind, so I slipped into the funnel from the south. It wasn't very long until deer starting coming through. Amazingly, this 11-point was the 28th deer, and third buck to come past me. He was too good to pass up. My .45 caliber muzzleloader did the job on him at 8:30 a.m."

That's How It Works

How would you like to be able to predict where most of the deer in your hunting area will travel? Would it help your hunt if you could see travel corridors even before you set foot in the woods? Would you like to make a list of potential stand sites without wandering around the woods looking for just the right spot? You can do it! You can predict deer movement patterns and know the routes even before you get into the woods. All you have to do is learn to read maps.

Deer hunters run the gamut—from those who have never before looked at a topographical, aerial or plat map, to those who have used them extensively. But the key to using these tools successfully is to understand which topographical features influence deer movement and know how to find them on your maps. In short, you need to know what you're looking for

The most useful tool, one enabling you to discover prime locations in which to ambush the buck of your dreams, is the topographical (topo) map. If you don't have a topo map, buy one. Between the U.S. Geological Survey and other various outlets detailed in Chapter 14 you can usually find all the maps and photos you'll need. And once you get a map a whole new world of deer hunting will be open to you.

Looking at a topo map for the first time, it may seem like a bunch of chicken scratching. But the symbols are really a very methodical and detailed means of showing almost exactly what a region looks like.

In much of the United States the most common topographical maps are the 7.5-minute topographic quadrangle maps. Each one covers roughly 60 square miles. These maps are compiled by aerial photographs taken by photogramettric methods, and are updated periodically, but not often. The maps are divided into sections and each section is one square mile. One square mile covers 640 acres. A half section contains 320 acres, a quarter section 160, and so forth. A half section is 1/2 mile by 1 mile, while a quarter section is 1/2 mile by 1/2 mile and a square 40-acre parcel is 1/4 mile by 1/4 mile.

The latitude (angular distance, measured in degrees, north or south from the equator) and longitude (angular distance, measured in degrees, east or west of the Prime Meridian) are listed on each map, along with the range and township information. Each section has a red number for identification purposes. Aerial maps and plat maps showing who owns the land both have these same latitude, longitude, range, township and section numbers listed, and they correspond exactly to the topographical map information.

This corresponding information is quite useful. I oftentimes use it to accurately identify where property lines run. I can easily see where the property lines are located by transferring ownership information from a plat map onto a topographical map. When I first leased land in southern Indiana four years ago I used this method to draw in all of the property lines on a topographical map. Since this information is so accurate, it's settled a few arguments about property line locations that I've had with those hunting on adjacent land.

In addition, if you have a Global Positioning System, all of the information can be utilized when you are using a GPS unit in your hunting. Some GPS units even have an over and under feature that can tell you on a topographical map exactly where you are standing on earth. It's all neat stuff.

The beautiful but vast hills in Wisconsin contain many trophy whitetails. Can you figure out how to hunt the region in a matter of days? You can if you use topographical maps.

TERRAIN TERMS

Funnels: A funnel is a narrow strip of cover, usually timber that connects two larger tracts of cover. When deer travel about during daylight hours they will use this strategic funnel to travel between the two large pieces of cover, so it "chokes" deer movement down close to your stand site. This funnel can be a narrow strip of woods between woodlots. It can also be a wide, timbered fencerow. Or it may be a strip of woods alongside a stream. There are many variations covered in this book. All are good locations to spend time in throughout the season. However, the tail end of the rut is the ultimate time to be on stand in a funnel because the bruiser bucks are out searching for the few remaining does still in estrus.

Inside and double inside corners: Inside and double inside corners are what I call half funnels. A farm field or pasture can sometimes form an "L" in timber it adjoins. This "L" shaped inside corner is easy to find on a map. Deer will stay in the woods and cut around these corners when traveling from one end of the woods to the other. Again, this funnels deer close to your stand. Inside corners are highly productive, but low key and often overlooked. Like true funnels, they are productive throughout the year, although the tail end of the rut will give you the best chance at a trophy in this location.

Saddles: Basically a saddle is a low spot in a ridgeline. Because it is low and usually narrow, it's the easiest travel route for a whitetail to use when going from one side of a hill to another Although a saddle can be found entirely within the timber in hilly regions, it forms a great funnel.. The more forest found on each side of the saddle, the more deer traffic it normally carries. Deer use saddles at all times of the day, but because they are often found deep within hilly regions the midday hunting in this position can be red-hot. Peak rut and the tail end of the rut will produce the most big buck sightings here. Cold late-season weather will keep deer up and moving through saddles, and dandy bucks can also be picked off when the temperatures drop.

Field saddles: These are low spots in open fields that hide deer from view of any nearby roads. It's a quick route whitetails can use to move from one piece of cover to another. While deer will use these field saddles at any time of the day, they will use them most frequently during the rut and especially, the tail end of the rut when they are traveling around a lot. Field saddles can be excellent during the midday hours.

Points: Points are found at the ends of ridges where they drop down to valleys or farm fields below. Deer in the hills often use these points as bedding areas. In addition, they also provide whitetails with perhaps the best terrain in which they can avoid hunters. Slipping from point to point — point hopping — allows a mature buck to avoid his pursuers, throwing them completely off track. Points are the most difficult terrain to learn when and how to hunt properly. Typically a deer trail follows along a hillside and will cross the point as it drops down. A deer trail on the opposite hillside usually crosses at this same location, as may a trail following the length of the top of the ridge. This creates a stand site offering great odds when hunting on a point. Excellent deer traffic is found on many points throughout the duration of the hunting seasons.

Breaklines: Breaklines are lines of demarcation between two types of adjoining, but different types of cover. An example would be the line where a clearcut meets an open wood. These lines will consistently produce deer. Breaklines are found in both hilly and flat regions and can be seen on aerial maps, but not topo maps. While deer will weave in and out of the heavy cover, the main trail will parallel the breakline. Numerous rubs and scrapes will be found along this main trail. The best hunting is found where the outermost trails out of the brush intersect the main trail. Breaklines carry very predictable deer movement throughout the seasons. Of course the rut is always good.

Hilltop field funnels: These funnels are formed when a creek from a valley below leads up near a field on high ground. Rather than cross the creek with its steep, hilly banks on each side, deer will naturally travel up to the hilltop field funnel and cross there. Here the wind is easy to use and the field enables the observant hunter to make an undetected entry to the stand. Big deer can be taken here through the entire rut. Does and lesser bucks can easily be picked off in this location any time during the season.

Benches: In hilly regions, flat areas of various widths are sometimes found on the sides of hills. These benches make for easy walking and whitetails use them when traveling from one area to another. Benches also serve as outstanding locations for bucks to place sign, so rubs and scrapes will normally be found there. A good understanding of the wind is needed to hunt benches. They carry excellent deer traffic throughout the year.

Converging hubs: Terrain that extend like spokes on a wheel create a converging hub. It's a looser choke point than a true funnel so the hunter using a firearm will find such areas most advantageous. In the hills, several ridges coming together typically form a converging hub. On flat land, several small streams converging in one location will form a great hub of deer activity. Hubs are excellent places to see deer movement throughout the season. In the hills be sure to look for favored oak trees in these hubs during early bow seasons. They can be dynamite hunting.

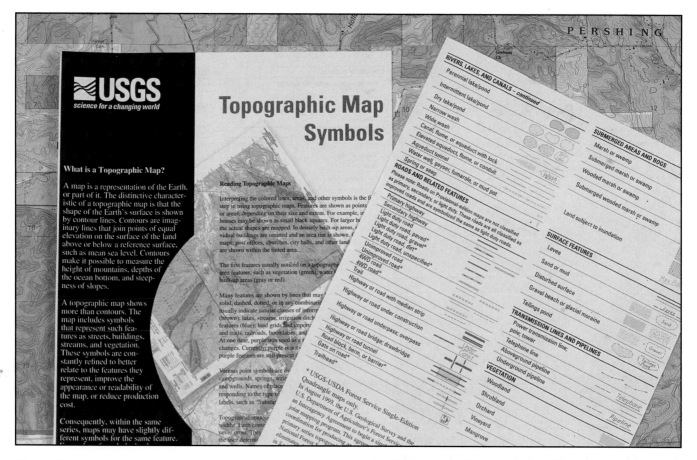

Sheets showing what each symbol on a topographical map stands for are available from the United States Geological Survey and several other companies.

Contour Lines: What They Can Tell You

Contour lines designate different elevations. Measurements are in feet above sea level. Contour lines on the 7.5-minute series topographic quadrangle maps are separated on 10-foot intervals, with a heavy accentuated line designating a 50-foot change in elevation. These lines essentially tell us what the terrain looks like. For example, 21 lines very close together show a steep hill with a 200-foot change in elevation. Whether it drops or rises is a matter of where you are standing when you look at the hill. With practice, we can identify hillsides, ridgetops, gullies, river bottoms, and all other features. And once we understand what these features look like on a map, the information will lead us to strategic deer hunting locations.

Imagining what contour lines are revealing about rises and drops in elevation is sometimes difficult for hunters to understand, especially those reading topographical maps for the first time. A topo map is a two-dimensional piece of paper, but must be viewed as a three-dimensional object. It takes some imagination, but try this: Take a 12-inch ruler or a yardstick and lay it down on your kitchen table. You can see the inch marker lines are spaced exactly 1 inch apart when the ruler is flat. Imagine these lines as contour lines on a topo map, each of them 10 feet apart. Make sure you are standing with the ruler or yardstick pointing away from you. Now grasp one end of the ruler or yardstick and start raising the end you are holding up in elevation while resting the other end on the table. As the ruler or yardstick gets higher, the lines will appear to get closer and closer together. As you can see, as the elevation contour lines get closer together the hillside gets steeper. Hold the ruler or yardstick straight up and you have a cliff.

Let's put this new knowledge into practice. If a topo map shows many contour lines close together, and then contour lines below this getting farther apart, you should be able to understand there is a steep hill which drops down in elevation quickly, then tapers off and drops more slowly.

By following contour lines on a topo map, you can also envision what geographic features look like in shape, as well as in elevation. For instance, contour lines running straight for a while, then bending around and almost coming back on themselves reveal we have a ridge running out and dropping down into a valley below. The end where it drops down is called a point. With a little practice, you'll get the hang of reading topographical maps, especially if you take them into a region you're already familiar with.

Other Map Features

On a topo map, small streams, rivers, swamps, ponds and lakes are designated by blue, while forested tracts are green. Open white regions normally are pastures and fields. Small black squares are houses, while small open squares are barns or other outbuildings. Any of these features that are shown in red have been added since the last time the map information was compiled. Most often, new features are houses, outbuildings, and ponds and lakes.

Each section on topographical maps, besides being numbered, are outlined with a fine red line. A fine dashed red line designates a fencerow. A heavy-duty road is shown as a thick, solid red line, while a medium duty road is shown as a thick, broken red line. Light-duty roads, such as gravel, are shown with two parallel black lines, and two dotted parallel black lines indicate an unimproved dirt lane. Each of these indicators are important because they can give you insight into how deer might act.

Perhaps you've found an inside corner, a feature that will be discussed at length later in the book, and want to place a stand there. Whitetails will usually stay inside the woods and closely skirt these inside corners when traveling during daylight hours. But if this corner is in a remote location, away from houses and roads, the deer may pop across the field before they get to the corner. This could influence your stand placement. If a house or road is nearby, activity in these locations helps keep the deer in the woods, causing them to funnel right by your stand position.

To take every advantage of the information a map offers you must give full consideration to every detail you see, because each can influence the movement of whitetails within a region. Each chapter in this book explains a different type of terrain feature to look for on a topo map, and with study you should be able to identify each one of these hot locations as you become a terrain strategist.

There is one aggravating thing you will run into once in a while when using topographical maps. You may, unfortunately, have a very interesting area you want to hunt and when you pull your topo maps out you find the spot you're interested in falls where four different map quadrangles come together. This means you have to cut the edges of four different maps, then tape them together to get a clear look of this topography. This used to be exasperating; but not any more. The Internet site www.mytopo.com has a feature that allows you to center the topo map quadrangle outline over the region you're interested in hunting, and order a custom layover. You can even have the map inscribed with your name on it, and order it waterproofed.

The Aerial Map

Aerial maps can serve the hunter with the habitat detail they show. Breaklines are formed in a timbered area when one section of the wood is logged, and another section is not. When you know what you are looking for on an aerial map, this breakline can be seen since the two different types of timber—mature trees and brush—will look different. The topo won't show this. Aerial maps are also helpful when you are studying fencerows. The topo map will show the fencerows as a fine, dashed red line, letting you know it is there. The aerial map will show if brush, or even large trees, are present in the fencerow, and if so, how much, where and how wide it is. This shows you the brushy fencerows whitetails use when traveling from one tract of

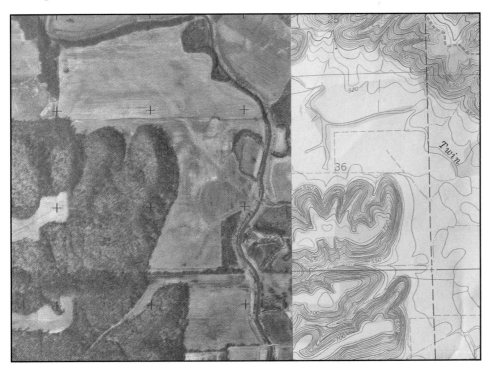

This picture shows the same area on both a topo and aerial map. As you can see, the aerial map shows much greater habitat detail such as brush, trees, and farm fields. The topo map, meanwhile, reveals the contour elevations very accurately to the trained eye.

timber to another and you don't even have to visit the land. From time to time you will even find converging hubs where several timbered fencerows come together.

Aerial maps also show field edges perfectly and will give you detail about the size of the timber there. Topo maps can be slightly off when mapmakers lay the green overlays representing forested areas on top of the contour lines. In some cases, a section of wood may have been logged and the area turned into a field or a field may have been abandoned and returned to short, thick undergrowth. A recent aerial map will reveal these changes better than a topo map.

Still, the vast majority of the time I use a topographical map to discover hot deer funnel locations. It's ideal for this because it tells me both the configuration of the terrain, and its elevations. The aerial map, even though it is an actual picture taken from above of the terrain you are interested in, is limited in some respects. It will show roads, houses, ponds, streams, and more. Depending on the lighting at the time the photograph was taken, you will even be able to see streams of all sizes in both flat and hilly regions. Some contour shapes may also be discernable to the trained eye, but the photo will not, however, show elevation changes. Moreover, this means that while you can find certain deer travel corridors such as inside corners and flat land funnels, you usually won't be able to identify such things as saddles in hilly regions.

Plat maps show the ownership of property within a county. They are useful in many ways.

So, the long and short of this is that it pays to use both aerial and topo maps to get the most information about a given piece of property.

Plat Map Usage

Typically plat maps are ordered by each county in order to show the ownership of each tract of land. Numerous companies and individuals use plat maps for a variety of reasons. Someone wanting to build a new home and who is looking for a piece of property to buy may use a plat map in order to locate the owner. Real estate agents use them extensively. So do farmers, surveyors, loggers, and a number of other people, including deer hunters.

If I'm scouting a new region, the first thing I do is check my plat map to determine who owns each piece of land. This speeds up the process of obtaining permission to hunt. Once I have permission to hunt, I then transfer the property lines of this land onto a topo map. This is easily done since each range, township, section number, and other pertinent data on a plat map corresponds exactly to the information on a topo and aerial map. I then know the exact boundaries of each tract

When looking for property to lease, go to the index in the back of a plat map book and scan over all the names of those owning property. If you see someone's name listed numerous times, you can bet they own a lot of land, so this is a good starting point in your search.

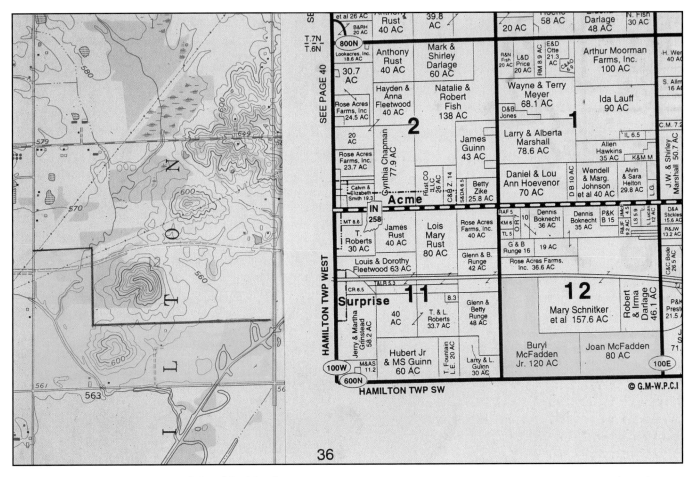

The Compass, Another Valuable Tool

Suppose that the next time you drive to work, you pay no attention to any of the stoplights. Instead of watching for the red, green, or yellow lights at each intersection, you simply drive right on through them, regardless of the color. Some of these lights you would breeze through without a problem because you would hit them on green. The stoplights on yellow wouldn't give you any problem, either. The lights on red would be an entirely different story. Other drivers would be locking up their brakes, sliding in all directions, blowing their horns, and in general trying to avoid you in any way they could. If you went through many stoplights, it would only be a matter of time until you crashed and burned.

Yes, stoplights facilitate traffic movement in a safe and time efficient way, assuring everyone gets to their destination in one piece.

Likewise, the compass serves as a stoplight for any prime deer-hunting bottleneck you might find on a topo or aerial map. If the perfect wind to hunt a deer funnel in the terrain should be from the south and the compass says it's out of the north, a red light should come on in your head. Stop. Don't hunt there. If the compass shows the wind coming from a southeasterly or southwesterly

By careful measuring, you can transfer property lines from a plat map to a topographical map. It's more accurate than you might think, and will help you determine hunting boundaries.

direction, this might mean a yellow, or caution, light comes on in your head. Be careful, watch out, and proceed only with caution. If the compass indicates the wind is coming directly from the south, obviously this is a green light. You can proceed with the hunt without any danger of being detected by a deer.

If you are smart enough to figure out all the key terrain features which deer might use in the topography of the land, yet hunt them without considering the direction of the wind, you will be like the guy driving through those intersections without looking at the stoplights. You'll win a few deer hunting skirmishes, and you'll lose a few. Most likely you'll lose two or three to every one you win. I don't know about you, but I don't like those odds.

By wisely using a compass, you can kick your opportunities for success up considerably. When I find a strategic location on a topo or aerial map, I lay the map out flat so it is facing north (north is always at the top of a map). I do this, of course, by using a compass to determine where north is located. Once the map is laid out, I place the compass on the map in each of my

INSIDE CORNER

*An inquisitive mind, a
topo map and a compass
still are the basics of
learning how to successfully
hunt mature whitetail bucks.*

*Once you find a good deer funnel,
the next step is to determine the
wind directions that will work best
for this placement.*

hot spots and this helps determine the wind directions
most favorable for a hunt in these positions. At the same
time I try to determine the best travel routes to get into
and out of my stand site.

A basic compass is adequate for deer hunting.
Knowing the wind direction is what you're after. More
elaborate compasses will allow you to shoot lines to
assist you in walking straight for long distances. Several
new digital compasses are now on the market. I
especially like the wrist models from Bushnell since I
can wear them like a watch. Instead of fishing in my
pocket or pack every time I want to determine a
direction, I can simply glance down at my digital wrist
compass and get both the wind direction and the time.

It also has a calendar, alarm clock and thermometer,
just like the hand-held model.

With Bushnell's Digital Navigation Systems Pro
Models, both the wrist and hand-held models also give
you barometer information, an altimeter reading, and a
simple weather forecaster. They even have a map light
on them. All this is useful, but the old basic compass
will still do the job.

Besides using the compass while searching for hot
spots on my map in the comfort of my home, I also,
when possible, like to walk to the exact location I have
marked. Once there, I stand with the compass in my
hand to see how the wind comes through the spot. This
is what I call fine-tuning the hunting position and can

By using a compass and a topographical map, you can shoot a surprisingly accurate property line boundary if you have a starting point such as a cornerstone.

reveal if a terrain feature nearby is influencing the wind. Although this can be done at any time, it's best done in post-season when disturbing the deer isn't an issue. Once on stand in a deer funnel, it's also a good idea to use your compass in order to see how the wind is working. This is especially important if you're experimenting with hunting the side of a hill or a gully bottom. Both are extremely difficult places to hunt because of the way the wind may switch directions. A compass can help you learn more about any hunting location.

Good Record Keeping Is Key

Date: December 12, 1986. **Day:** Friday. **Hunt:** Morning. **Hours on stand:** 3. **Wind direction:** Directly from west. **Temperature:** 12 degrees to 23 degrees and sunny. **Map quadrangle:** Vallonia, Indiana. **Hunting Location:** Section 2, The High Saddle.

This information is from a simple diary I kept during the 1986 deer hunting season. One hundred years from now, you could take this same information, look at the

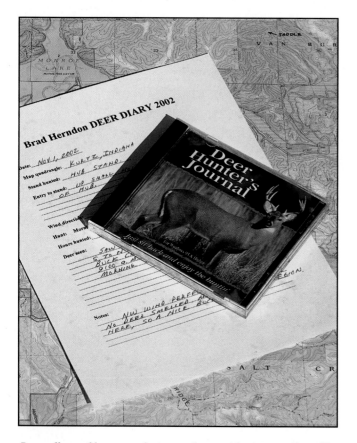

Regardless of how you do it, good record keeping will enable you to become a much better whitetail hunter. Stand names, wind directions, number of deer seen, and other pertinent data all will come in handy as you advance in your deer hunting skills.

Vallonia quadrangle I marked in 1986 and walk directly to the strategic saddle I hunted. By reading my entries about that day's hunt you would also learn I saw seven whitetails, none antlered. I even threw in some feelings concerning my general mood about life.

Accurate record keeping, like skilled map reading, will help you fill your deer tag year after year with the whitetail of your choice. I feel it is extremely important to name each of your stands, record their exact locations on your map, and mark which wind directions can be effectively used while hunting each stand. An Iowa hunting trip Carol and I made a few years back will prove the value of record keeping.

We were hunting in south central Iowa near the town of Keosauqua during archery season. Keosauqua contained the only lodging in the county, and we were staying in an old motel that had been built as an addition behind an even older hotel. The old hotel had an American flag on top and if the wind was blowing, Old Glory revealed the direction.

Interestingly, in my deer hunting travels, this hunt was the only time I couldn't pick up a National Weather Service station on my weather radio. Calling around, I made a contact with a nice fellow who worked in the control tower of an airfield in the general area. Each morning when I got up, I would call him and he would tell me the predicted wind direction for the day. For a double check, I sometimes would step out of the room to look at the flag.

As I did this early one morning, I noticed a familiar looking fellow step out of an adjoining room. He, too, was looking up at the flag. "Mark! Mark Drury," I said. "What are you doing here?"

"We're up here bow hunting for some big whitetails," he replied. "I just came out to check the wind direction. Come in the room and talk a while."

Mark, Tad Brown and I had a good conversation for a few minutes before we went hunting, and I was very impressed with their preparations. Mark and his brother Terry are known for their in-the-wild deer hunt videos, and I always felt they were intelligent in the way they hunted.

Mark said they had hunted the region for several years and knew it well. He had every stand position named and marked, and the best wind direction for each location was also recorded. Within a few days, they had filled their archery tags with nice bucks and headed home with considerable video footage.

This was a classic example of how detailed record keeping pays off. Record every detail of every stand location where you spend time and you never have to wonder about which stand placement "might" be right.

By using topo and aerial maps—and a little shoe leather—you can discover all of the strategic deer ambush locations listed here. You can accurately place rub and scrape locations on a topo map should you desire to do so.

The Weather Radio:
Don't Leave Home Without It.

I need three things to plan my deer hunting strategy: A topo map, a compass and a weather radio. It would be hard for me to deer hunt without using all three of these important tools. The weather radio, at first glance, might seem to be the item I could do without since weather forecasts can now be picked up on the Internet or the Weather Channel on TV. The disadvantage to gathering the weather forecast from these two sources is that neither of them is very portable. The weather radio, fortunately, can be taken with you.

Even on the land we lease here in Indiana, the weather radio dictates which stands we will be able to use for each morning and evening hunt. Our weather radio is easy to carry and powered by a 9-volt battery. The range of this particular radio is about 60 miles or so. Usually picking up a National Weather Service radio station isn't a problem. That hunt I talked about in Iowa was the exception to the rule.

The National Oceanic and Atmospheric Administration (NOAA) Weather Radio (NWR) is a nationwide network of radio stations broadcasting continuous weather information directly from regional National Weather Service offices. NWR broadcasts National Weather Service warnings, watches, forecasts and other hazard information 24 hours a day. In our region we can pick up three weather radio stations. Louisville, Kentucky, 60 miles away; Bloomington,

Even after he's on stand, the author checks the wind to see how it's working for the location. He then notes in a diary the best wind directions for this particular stand site.

An inexpensive weather radio will keep you informed of the wind directions in your hunting area 24 hours per day.

Indiana, 35 miles away; and Seymour, Indiana, 10 miles away.

On a typical morning deer hunt, we get up and get ready, then check out the wind direction predictions from every nearby weather radio station. The wind direction and speed determines our stand positions for the day. We have about a 35-mile drive to get to the county where we most often hunt. The drive takes about 45 minutes. Once we arrive at our hunting destination, we once more check the predicted wind direction on our weather radio to make sure it hasn't changed. Most of the time the wind direction remains the same, but not always. I have seen the wind direction prediction change 90 degrees during this 45-minute drive. One thing you will quickly learn when you start using a weather radio and studying weather fronts closely, is that weather predicting is a very inexact science, even with all the modern technology now available.

Weather radios can be purchased in a number of stores. Ours came from Radio Shack. All other major electronics

Some sporting goods stores, National Forest headquarters, and other places carry topographical maps. For best results contact USGS Information Services, Box 25286, Denver, CO 80225, phone 888-275-8747, fax 303-202-4693. Their Web site is www.usgs.gov. On their Web site, click on "Online Maps and Photos", which will be found under "Explore Our Products and Data." This will take you to "View USGS Maps and Aerial Photo Images Online."

Plat books showing the ownership of the property in the county you desire to hunt usually can be obtained at the county courthouse in that county. Many local county Farm Bureau Cooperatives and some banks also carry them. They can even be ordered from the printer selling them to the county. You can also use a search engine on the Internet to find various suppliers of plat books. Simply type "plat book" into the search engine.

Weather radios can be purchased at various retailers specializing in electronics. They provide hourly weather predictions for your locality, including accurate wind directions, and should be a tool used daily by every serious whitetail hunter. Prices range from $20 to $50 or more if you want to get elaborate.

retailers also carry them, as well as some department stores and drug stores. They can also be purchased through mail order catalogs carrying hunting equipment.

There are two grades of weather radios: residential-grade and commercial-grade. Residential grade weather radios vary in price from $20 to $200. Commercial-grade weather radios run from hundreds of dollars to thousands of dollars. Residential-grade weather radios will serve your needs quite well. While they are valuable in deer hunting, you will also find yourself using weather radios when you are turkey hunting, fishing and planning a camping trip. We also use a weather radio extensively in our photography work.

Staying On Stand

By learning how to read topographical and aerial maps, you can find terrain features deer will use regularly as they move about. The compass, used in conjunction with the map, will tell you what wind direction will best serve your needs. And the weather radio will tell you when the wind you need is in the forecast. When all this comes together as it should, you have assembled the perfect hunt. Yet, despite this attention to detail you are not yet assured of success. There is more you must do.

Having your stand in the most strategic location in your entire hunting area, with an ideal wind caressing your face, won't do you much good if you can't stay on stand until Mr. Big comes trotting along. Learning to dress properly will enable you to stay on stand long enough to make the best use of all the information you have gathered and processed.

Even in this day and age I still talk to far too many hunters who "freeze out" and go home early. Their stories bring back cold, painful memories. When I started deer hunting in the late 1960s, I was poor. On brisk mornings I put on several thin shirts for insulation, and the one heavy coat I had. Two pair of pants, an old hat, brown jersey gloves, several layers of work socks, and a pair of thin, cheap boots topped off my hunting

Learn how to dress properly so you can stay on stand as long as you need to. It doesn't do you any good to have a great ambush location, and then freeze out at 10 a.m.

attire. If the morning temperature was down around 30 degrees, 8:30 a.m. found me in severe pain. By 9:00 a.m. I was out of there, glad to be alive.

I've often wondered what kind of bucks walked past some of my stands after I had vacated them. Maybe you have had the same thoughts about some of your whitetail hunts.

Live (freeze) And Learn

Through many years of whitetail hunting, Carol and I have learned what it takes to stay on stand in all kinds of weather. Cold, wind, rain, snow, you name it, and we now can hang in there when the weather is at its worst. And best of all, we're warm and dry enjoying the day of deer hunting, just as we're supposed to. We haven't tried every product out there. We simply have come up with a formula that works for us, so we stick to it. Don't ever be afraid to experiment with clothing, boots, and other products.

I consider dressing properly a tool of the trade, and so should you. On moderately cold days I start off with a bottom layer of Damart insulated underwear. It's thin, comfy, and comes in five grades of warmth. Putting Damart on gives me the same feeling I had when I used to put on my new school clothes in the fall. It makes me feel good. I normally use Grade 3 Damart, unless it's a brutally cold day. Next comes a regular pair of camo pants and a shirt. On my feet I wear a pair of wool socks, or a wool mix of some type. If the day isn't too cold, a

The use of an umbrella will allow you to hunt even in rainy weather. The umbrella shown here is a commercial model, but an inexpensive umbrella can be altered and works extremely well.

Hands and feet get cold fast. Quality pac boots will make sure you have warm feet and this will add to an enjoyable hunting experience.

WIND CHILL CHART

To use the Wind Chill Chart locate the temperature on the top row, and the estimated wind speed in the left-hand column. Where the two intersect in the chart is the wind chill temperature. Pay careful attention to wind chill temperatures. Most people who die from hypothermia do so on days when the air temperature is not brutally cold. Be prepared by wearing or carrying enough clothes with you. And remember: A person loses over half of his body heat from the neck and head area.

Wind Speed	Air Temperature (degrees Fahrenheit)									
	40	35	30	25	20	15	10	5	0	-5
5mph	36	31	25	19	13	7	1	-5	-11	-16
10mph	34	27	21	15	9	3	-4	-10	-16	-22
15mph	32	25	19	13	6	0	-7	-13	-19	-26
20mph	30	24	17	11	4	-2	-9	-15	-22	-29
25mph	29	23	16	9	3	-4	-11	-17	-24	-31
30mph	28	22	15	8	1	-5	-12	-19	-26	-33

moderately insulated pair of hunting boots goes on over these socks. A standard hat and lightweight gloves finish off the ensemble.

This is all I normally wear when I walk in to my stand. At times I may wear a lightweight jacket or heavier jacket on top depending on the weather conditions. What I'm doing here—and this is important—is keeping my body from working up a sweat as I walk in. Sweating profusely can really put a chill on your body once you get on stand, especially if you use insulated products that don't wick moisture away from your body.

To avoid sweating on the way to stand, Carol uses a lightweight, but spacious backpack to carry in the rest of her clothing and other hunting paraphernalia. What is contained in her pack varies with the time of year and the type of deer hunting she is doing. I'll mention most everything she carries, although keep in mind these products can be added or deleted as necessary.

Included in her pack will be a pair of insulated coveralls, an insulated 3/4-length jacket, a Damart balaclava, one Damart facemask and another extra facemask. In addition, she will have one pair of Damart fingerless gloves and one pair of fingered gloves, a hooded sweatshirt, a warm hat, and an umbrella and bungee cords. We both always carry a cheap umbrella from one of the discount stores in our pack, regardless of the weather.

In order for these umbrellas to work properly, we cut out the back portion of the umbrella so it will fit the contour of an average tree. If it rains or snows, we simply use the bunge cords to quickly attach the umbrella to the tree. This may seem like a redneck setup, but an inexpensive umbrella is lightweight and works extremely well. While using this custom umbrella we've taken several dandy deer on rainy days, and we've stayed high and dry. Commercially made hunting umbrellas also are available and we certainly recommend using an umbrella of some type. It's just this simple: You must stay on stand in order to get a crack at a trophy deer, or any deer for that matter.

Also in Carol's pack will be found a flashlight, chemical hand warmers, a bow vest in archery season, safety belt, compass, grunt call, rattling box, knife, high-energy snacks, extra pull-up string, and screw-in hooks to hold her binoculars or other items. She also has fire-starting materials, a whistle and small strobe light in case she is stranded in the woods. She makes a point to leave her survival items at the base of the tree. If it's a horribly rainy day, she will have a good lightweight rain suit along.

When it gets extremely cold, we switch over to good pac boots with felt liners and wear two pair of wool socks. We make sure that we never get our feet too tight in the boots since this close contact with the outer boot will conduct heat more easily to the outside. In cold, damp weather we often wear wool pants and wool shirts. If it gets bitterly cold we will sometimes go to another grade of Damart or even two layers. Whatever it takes to stay warm, we do it.

Going back to the bow vest Carol carries, it's an item

BINOCULARS ARE A MUST

Quality binoculars are a must for locating and field judging deer. Buy the best optics you can afford. You'll be glad you did.

Binoculars should be required for every whitetail hunter. They enable you to field judge bucks at a distance; allow you to make sure you are shooting a doe rather than a button buck when reducing your deer herd, and are handy for checking out many other fascinating details in the woods. Your age will determine what size binoculars to buy. For example, in total darkness a young person's pupils will dilate (open) to about 8mm. That's about 3/10 of an inch. At age 40 an eye's pupil will dilate to only 6mm; at 50 it's 5mm; 4mm at 60; and the pupil will dilate to only 2mm at age 80.

If you're under 40 you will be best served using binoculars with 6mm or 7mm exit pupils since your eyes can use all the light the binoculars will deliver to you. You determine the exit pupil diameter of a binocular by dividing the objective lens diameter by the power (a 7x42 binocular would have a 6mm exit pupil).

A good choice for those under 40 would be binoculars in the 6x42, 7x42, 7x50, 8x50, 8x56 and 10x70 range. Older hunters could use these just mentioned binoculars, of course, but their pupils wouldn't open up enough to use all of the light delivered to their eyes. Something in the 6x30, 8x32, 7x35, 8x42, 10x42 and 10x50 range would work well for them. I don't recommend using the 8x20, 8x24 or 10x25 range of binoculars since they produce unduly dark images in low light.

When purchasing a pair of binoculars, buy the best glass you can afford in a weight you can live with carrying. I use quality 7x42 and 8x42 binoculars and they work well. Center-focusing models with diopter adjustments allow you to refocus frequently. If you wear eyeglasses, you'll need extra-long eye relief in your binoculars, at least 15mm to 20mm.

hardly anyone ever uses—or even knows about. Again, although it may seem like another gimmick, the bow vest is an item she always uses, both in hot and cold weather. The bow vest simply slips on over your outer clothes. An open pouch in the vest near your crotch is where the bottom limb of the bow rests. At chest level, a Z clip slips around the bowstring. Once this clip is in place, you let go of your bow and it hangs in front of you with the arrow on the string. This allows you to have your hands free, and since this setup doesn't put any undue weight on any part of your body, it's very comfortable.

When you see a deer coming, it's a simple matter to slowly grip your bow, tip it back slightly, which allows the Z clip to silently drop away, and you're ready to shoot.

I still hear stories every year about archers grabbing for their bow on the side of the tree, and in the process this movement catches the eye of an approaching deer, scaring it off. The bow vest assures your bow is ready without any undue movement. Amazingly, the bow vest can also be used when sitting down.

Like Carol, I also walk in to my deer stand sites with light clothing on.

And also like Carol, when I get to the tree I put on whatever other clothes I feel are needed for the hunt. My setup for carrying extra clothes and other items is somewhat different than hers. I carry a 6-1/2-pound Free Spirit Loc-On tree stand. It serves as a frame for a special pack I attach to it. This pack is lightweight and spacious and will hold all of my extra gear. This is a great setup, allowing me to either use a stand already in place, or to erect the stand I have carried in. I carry several rope-on steps with me and because my stand is equipped with a speed-rope, I can have it up and be in it in seven or eight minutes.

The equipment I carry is almost identical to Carol's items except that I carry a urine bottle and a rangefinder at times. Regarding restroom breaks, Carol has good advice. "In deer season, never drink more than one half cup of coffee in the morning."

Another neat little item we both carry is a call holder that attaches to the wrist with Velcro. It holds two calls. We can grunt, bleat, or do both simultaneously, even at full draw. No lanyards in the way to catch on a bowstring, no putting a call back in the pocket, just call and shoot. Moreover, these calls are used infrequently since our high-odds stand sites usually funnel deer directly past us.

Of All The Things I've Lost......

Not too long ago a man was talking to me about the problem he had with losing items. "Of all the things I've lost," he said, "I miss my mind the most."

Just when you think you've got it all figured out, a topo map can reveal to you a previously overlooked strategic terrain feature that deer frequently use.

Your mind is the most important terrain tool you have at your disposal. Use it wisely.

A good work ethic will give you the determination to study maps of all kinds. A curious mind will enable you to probe each nook and cranny of the land where you hunt. Attention to detail will allow you to decipher what those maps are telling you about the terrain, leading you to discover the hottest terrain features deer will use. Patience will enable you to wait for the exact wind direction. And persistence will keep you on stand enough for you to be successful. This, in turn, will build up your confidence and make all of your hunts more enjoyable, regardless of the results.

It's up to you to assemble and intelligently use all of the tools of the terrain trade I have listed in this chapter. I have faith that you have the abilities to do the job well.

He's nailed you! You'll take more and bigger bucks than you thought possible once you learn how to hunt so the wind is always in your favor—or at least as much as possible.

Chapter 2

Mastering the Wind
A Key To
Success

By 1983 I had a good understanding of how deer use the terrain, and was able to locate strategic travel corridors. One such place was a small valley meandering south for roughly 2 miles. The terrain then rose to a large flat plateau. The hillsides on each side of this valley were hardwoods and bordered a long field running the length of the valley bottom. About half way up this field was a timbered thicket that connected the hillsides on each side of the farm field. Of course whitetails used this connecting thicket heavily when out traveling from one hillside to the other during daylight hours.

Knowing this, and having had the exciting experience of seeing a buster buck, in the same region while grouse hunting the year before; I began hunting this deer funnel when the rut kicked in during early November. Each morning I would listen to the wind direction on my weather radio to determine my stand site. It was a simple task to walk up the middle of the field and slip into my chosen location.

From the time I started hunting this funnel I noticed the wind changed a lot. First it would come from the predicted direction, then just minutes later it would change to an entirely different direction. At times the wind would blow from four different directions within a 30-minute period. Naturally deer coming through this funnel winded me from time to time and spooked. Still, I thought I could get "lucky" and when Mr. Big came cruising through the wind would be in my favor and I would pick him off.

Around 9:30 a.m. one mid-November morning I heard footsteps in the crisp dry leaves southeast of my stand. Hoping it would be the buck I was pursuing, I turned my attention in that direction. While moving into position, I noted that the wind was perfect. As the steps came closer, my heart raced. Then the steps stopped; the woods were silent. Ever so slightly I could feel a breeze on the back of my neck. The wind had changed. Shortly I heard footsteps again. Only they weren't coming towards me; the deer was going the other way.

The deer backtracked to a small point that meandered up the hill to the east. Once there the whitetail slowly walked up the point to the top of the hill. I watched with a sick feeling as glimpses of the deer revealed huge antlers bobbing through the woods. Yes, it was the trophy buck I was after and he had nailed me, thanks to the changing wind.

Carol Herndon has taken several excellent bucks from an inside corner the author overlooked in 1983. Through trial and error, Brad learned that hunting high ground in hilly regions will result in a much higher success rate on trophy whitetails.

What I Learned

Although I knew deer had an acute sense of smell, this hunt was a turning point in how I selected stand sites. While watching the trophy whitetail walk away from me was discouraging, it made me wonder how many deer had winded me when the woods were wet. This meant I couldn't have heard them walking and they could have silently slipped away from me undetected. I finally realized I should avoid hunting in low gullies in hilly regions, and to also avoid side-of-the-hill tree stand sites. Every low creek valley I hunted in and every stand I used on the side of a hill, ended up presenting me with variable winds throughout the day, making my chances of success very low.

I decided to start hunting only high ground in hilly regions until I gained much more experience in mastering the wind. This was not to say I completely gave up on hunting some of these difficult stand sites. Later on, when my understanding of the wind was better I would once more put time in on stand in some of these locations. But at that point in my hunting career, I was content to hunt high and dry. In hilly regions, you should do the same until you become an expert at mastering the wind. **Remember: You can't change the wind. But you can understand how the wind changes.**

Spraying powder to determine wind direction will help you to understand how wind flows in hilly regions.

When hunting a hilly region, understanding how thermals work within this type of terrain will be instrumental in how many successful hunts you make, especially if you're a bow hunter.

Hunting On Top Has Advantages

When hunting flat land a deer hunter doesn't have to worry much about changing wind directions. If the weather forecast is for a steady west wind, the hunter can enter a wood from the east, place his stand downwind of a strategically located deer trail in a funnel and be in business. Hilly regions are not so easy. Down low, the wind changes directions, and will even swirl. On the side of a steep hill the wind will switch back and forth quite often. I'll discuss why this happens a little later in this chapter and how you can still use the wind—under the right conditions—in these locations. For now let's see why hunting high in the hills will fill deer tags and occasionally produces a megabuck.

After the buck mentioned above escaped me, I started hunting another region of public land near my home and did not return for several years to the site where the wind betrayed me. When I did return, I had learned the value of hunting on the high ground in hilly regions and had an entirely different perspective of what to look for regarding tree stand locations.

Although I didn't know it at the time, in 1983 when I watched the trophy buck's antlers bob up the point toward the top of the hill, the deer, once it reached the level land on top, actually walked right through an inside corner. It's

Once you understand how the wind works in the hills, your success rate on deer of all sizes will go up considerably.

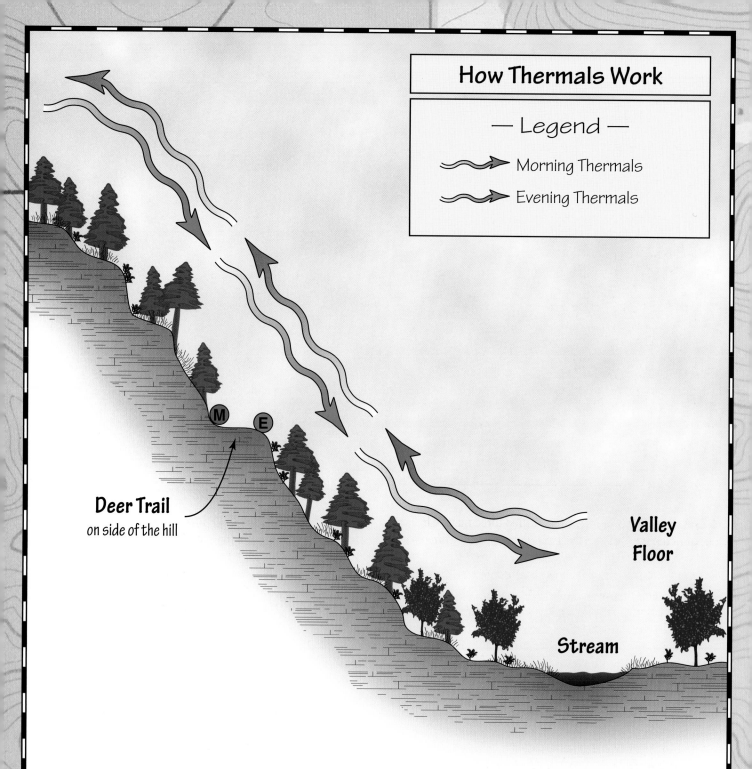

How Thermals Work

— Legend —

Morning Thermals

Evening Thermals

Deer Trail
on side of the hill

Valley Floor

Stream

Shown here is a cross-section view of a typical small valley in the hills. What we have done is cut the valley in two, and we are looking at one hillside and the valley floor. The red morning arrows show how thermals rise in the morning on a calm day, meaning you can come in from the top of the hill and hunt above the side of the hill deer trail. On a calm evening, the air cools, dropping back down the hillside, as the green evening arrows show. This allows you to enter from the valley floor and position a tree stand below the hillside deer trail.

Also keep in mind that a deer trail at the very top of a hill can be effectively hunted using these morning and evening thermals as well. Neither of these thermals work for hunting down low, however, when the winds are brisk and vary in wind velocity.

ILL. 2.1

Even though this 10-point buck isn't a monster, missing P & Y by more than 3 inches, it's still a deer the author is proud of. Extremely sick during most of the 2000 deer hunting season, Herndon took this deer on January 7, 2001. He shot it on the last day of deer season, the last evening, and in the last 10 minutes of shooting light. Don't give up!

the same inside corner Carol has killed three mature bucks out of in the past four years! Isn't it amazing the difference a few years of additional knowledge will make?

On ridgetops, flat plateaus, and other types of high ground in hilly regions, the wind generally stays constant. This allows you to obtain the predicted wind direction for the day, make an intelligent entry to stand, and remain there undetected by the deer for hours on end. Besides inside corners on high ground, saddles, hilltop field funnels, and converging hubs are also great places to bag mature whitetails. With a little thought and great patience, you should be able to work with the wind in each of these positions and experience excellent success.

And once you have learned to use the wind in these stand positions in your favor, you can key in on other placements that are more difficult to hunt; such as those dreaded gullies and hillsides. To fill tags in these areas, it will take an understanding of the wind that goes well beyond the basics.

Using Thermals To Your Advantage

On a calm, cool, but sunny morning, the sides of a valley in a hilly region will heat up, creating an upward thermal. This condition will allow you to effectively come in from a ridgetop and place your stand above a hillside deer trail. Your scent will be lifted up and away from the deer

trail in front of you, allowing you to hunt undetected for possibly two or three hours. As the temperature rises the wind will pick up and possibly start to change, so be aware that effective thermal hunts may be short.

The same conditions will work great on a morning hunt in a hilltop field funnel. Entering from a field, you can hunt a tree stand placed between the field and where the deer trail skirts around the top of the creek near the top of the hill. Because the day is calm and warming, the air within the gully will warm and flow up the streambed, sweeping your scent right back out in the field. Again, if the morning is supposed to be calm, this hunt may be short-lived because when the air temperature soars, the wind will pick up and may not be favorable for your site. Still, you have made a perfect hunt for a few hours and oftentimes that's all it takes.

On warm sunny days that calm down in the evening, you can come up a valley floor and hunt below a hillside deer trail since the cooling air will be dropping back into the gully. The hilltop field funnel can't be hunted in this situation since some deer typically walk along the length of the stream to the top of the hill, loop around the end of the stream at the hilltop field funnel, and then drop back down the hill. These deer would most likely wind you because the cooling thermal sucks your scent down the streambed. **Illustration 2.1** shows how thermals work in a typical small valley on a calm morning and evening hunt.

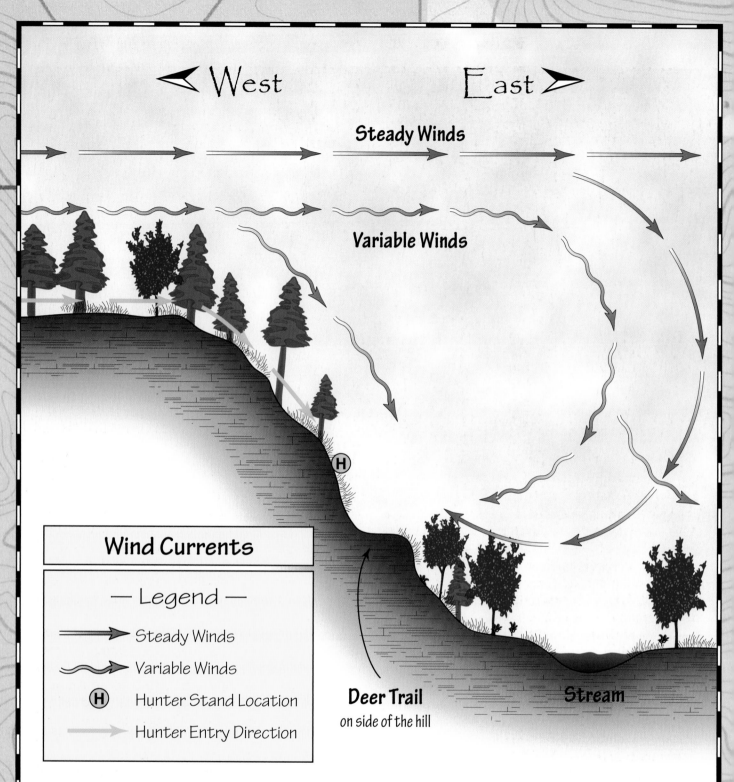

◄ West **East ►**

Steady Winds

Variable Winds

Wind Currents

— Legend —

→ Steady Winds

〰➤ Variable Winds

Ⓗ Hunter Stand Location

→ Hunter Entry Direction

Deer Trail
on side of the hill

Stream

Moderate to high winds, unless they are of a steady velocity, make hunting in a valley bottom or on the side of a hill unproductive because the wind is constantly switching back and forth all day. By looking at the variable winds, you can see how they flow from the west, swirl east and back west. As related in the story, the steady 15 mph wind the author used curled around and came back up the hill. The author was able to hunt productively with this wind until noon, passing up some small deer who were unaware of his presence.

Learning how the wind reacts down low in the hills can only truly be acquired through reading, and then in-the-field experience. Understanding how the wind reacts under these conditions, and how you can effectively use it is one of deer hunting's most difficult challenges.

ILL. 2.2

Even after you've learned to master the wind, check your equipment occasionally throughout the hunting season to make sure it's in tip top shape.

There's another hilly terrain feature down low that you might want to consider for an evening hunt when the thermal conditions are right. This is found when you have a small hollow coming from a ridgetop and the mouth of the hollow ends at the edge of a farm field or pasture below. For example, the fall of 1999 was one of the warmest and driest in history in much of the United States. Most days were breezy, but calmed down just before dark. Because the days were hot, as the sun set in the evening, tremendous downward thermals were formed, actually creating a slight wind coming out the ends of the small timbered hollows where they joined farm fields such as I just described.

Waiting until late evening, I used these cooling thermals to make several perfect hunts that fall, in the process almost picking off a great buck. Unfortunately, in my excitement I moved a little too quickly and the rascal buck, up on the hill above me, saw me move. It seems I never learn some lessons well enough. What I'm saying, though, is great hunts can be made down low if you know how to use the wind beyond the basics.

Understanding Vacuums

Instead of a calm wind, let's now examine how winds of higher speed flow down low in hilly regions, especially on the sides of hills. Looking at **Illustration 2.2** you will see how winds coming over the top of a hill create a vacuum as the wind changes speeds. In other words, with changing wind velocities all day, the wind will switch direction 180 degrees throughout the day. This is a no-win situation. A steady wind, however, is another matter.

Again, I will share another hunt I made one fall. The wind prediction of the day was from the west, and steady at 15 miles per hour. In one region I hunt there is a deer trail running along the side of a moderately sloping hill approximately 100 feet in height. Because of decades of thinking about the wind, and experimenting, I was relatively sure the steady 15 mph west wind would curl back and change directions completely.

As I entered stand shortly before daylight on the west side of the deer trail — the wrong side to normally be with a west wind — the wind changed back and forth for a short period of time. Shortly, the wind picked up and remained steady, and the vacuum formed by it coming over the top of the hill produced an ideal east wind for me the rest of the morning. A few years back I wouldn't have had the nerve, or knowledge, to try a gamble of this nature.

When trying difficult hunts of this type, remember wind flows over terrain differently, depending on the size of the land, the height of the hill, and other factors. Mastering how to hunt down low is a life-long learning process and much of it comes from keeping careful notes about each hunt, the wind direction and speed, and the layout of the land.

Sea Breezes

Although I don't live or hunt near a large body of water, simply out of interest I have studied weather data

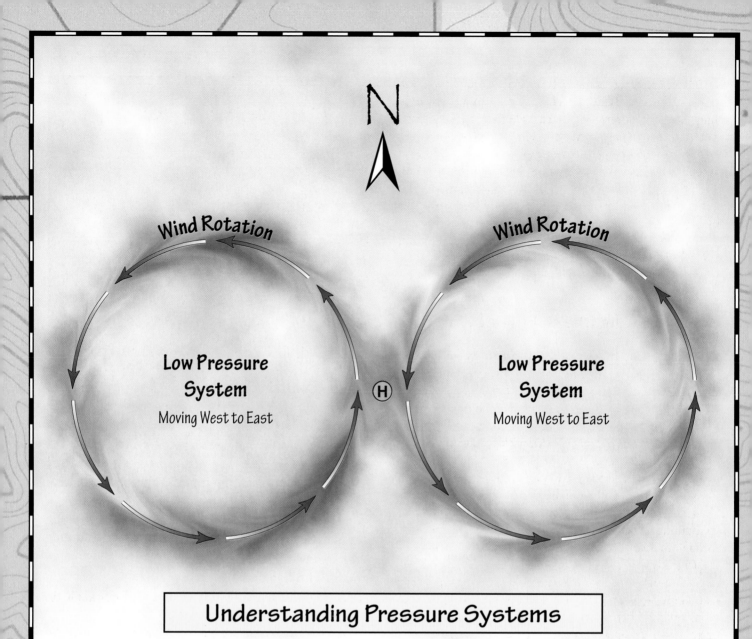

N

Wind Rotation

Wind Rotation

Low Pressure System

Moving West to East

Ⓗ

Low Pressure System

Moving West to East

Understanding Pressure Systems

This illustration shows how a low pressure system, traveling from the west to the east creates an undesirable south wind when the system is to the west of you. As it travels east, however, the wind where you are at changes gradually, coming from the southeast, east, northeast, and finally from the north. This happens because as the front moves, you are placed in different positions in relation to it, even though you have never actually moved. You can understand from the discussion in our story how you could start hunting your strategic stand site in the travel corridor as soon as the wind changed even slightly to from the northeast. Of course it only gets better after that as it comes more from the north.

Remember a low pressure system has a counterclockwise wind rotation, while a high pressure system has a clockwise wind rotation direction. It takes study to figure out this wind switching that high and low pressure systems cause, but you will be able to master it with time and experience.

ILL. 2.3

and have gathered some information about how large bodies of water affect the wind. Some of you who may hunt near the ocean, the Great Lakes, or another large body of water should find this information useful

On calm mornings and evenings you can predict wind directions relatively well in these localities. Over water, the air is not heated very much (the water absorbs the heat), while over land the air is heated more quickly. Because of this, on a calm morning wind directions will flow from over the water toward the land. In the evening, breezes move from the land out over the water. This little trick can help you put your tree stand in the right place

The Worst Wind Direction Prediction

Using a realistic, but made up example, consider what you might do in one of hunting's trickiest situations. Let's assume you're running out of time to waylay a bruiser buck you've been pursuing. Getting up early one morning near the end of deer season, you flip on the weather station on your TV and it says there has been a south wind all night, but it will switch and be coming from the north around noon. The south wind is horrible for your best stand site, but the north wind at noon is perfect. The question at this point is: At what time can you go hunting and be assured the wind will be in your favor enough to give you great odds of success?

This is one of a deer hunter's greatest dilemmas; hearing the wind is going to switch, but you are unable to determine how it is going to switch. Will it change directions, going from south, to east, to north, or will it go from south, to west, to north? Being able to determine how the directional change of the wind occurs has a tremendous effect on whether you will be successful hunting or not. Let's examine the situation and see if I can get you on the right track to understanding wind rotation.

The first thing you should do in this situation is determine whether you have a low pressure or high pressure system moving through your area. High-pressure systems are associated with a rising barometer, while low pressure systems are associated with a falling barometric pressure. Next determine in what direction the front is traveling. Weather reports from various sources can tell you this. In the Midwest where I live most of our fronts come out of some westerly direction. Generally speaking, wind around high pressure turns clockwise, while wind around low pressure turns counterclockwise.

Going back to our weather forecast, let's assume the weather station said the wind that will be changing from south to north is associated with a low-pressure system, one moving from west to east. Remember the wind related to a low rotates counterclockwise. **Illustration 2.3**

An awesome deer trail snaking down to a standing cornfield that draws quantities of deer late in the season. Proceed with caution! If you try hunting down low near this field, you better know what you're doing.

shows the wind would most likely change from south, to southeast, to east, to northeast, to north.

What I have described here is very simplified compared to what actually happens in the world of weather. Whether the front is high pressure or low pressure, which direction it is moving, and where it is located in relation to where you hunt all affect how the winds will change. Still, if you study the rotational directions of high and low pressure, you will gain in your understanding of how to use the wind properly.

Sometimes little bits of knowledge like this seem insignificant. Yet in every region of the country there are whitetail hunters who, year in and year out, succeed where others fail. Talk to most of them and you will find they understand wind movement to a great degree. This is knowledge that is instrumental in their success rates. I'm sure if you put forth an honest effort in learning about the flow of the wind in your hunting region, you will see your confidence levels soar when you go deer hunting. And not only that, you will see the number and size of the bucks you tag increase substantially. In all likelihood you will find some of your best deer will fall to your arrow or bullet when you have been able to use the wind beyond the basics.

Chapter 3

The Perfect
Funnel

On flat land, both the topographical and aerial map will reveal where perfect funnels are located within the terrain you're hunting.

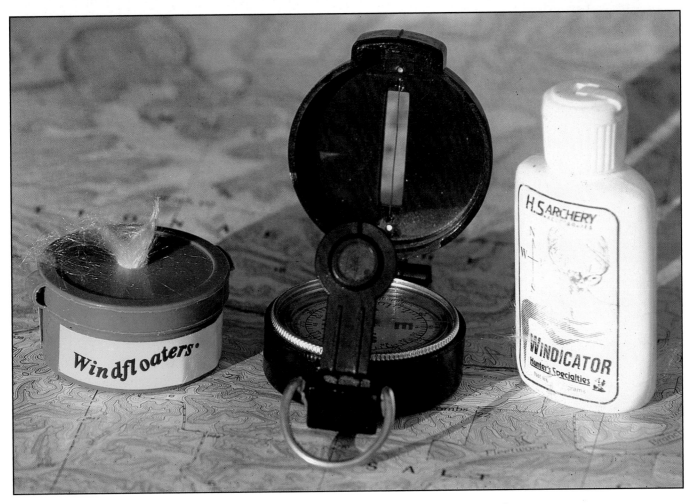

A compass and some type of wind indicator are extremely useful when hunting trophy whitetails.

It was November 23, 1981. Shortly before the break of day, legendary whitetail strategist Jay Mellencamp parked his vehicle along a county road and made his way across a harvested soybean field. After walking about half a mile, he silently slipped into a brushy section of timber dotted with mature trees. The tract of timber was about 80 yards wide. More importantly, it connected two vast sections of woods that lay east and west of this narrow strip of trees and brush.

After quietly screwing in his tree steps, Mellencamp soon had his stand positioned in a hardwood tree. After slipping on his insulated coveralls, he pulled up the .54 caliber muzzleloader he had recently completed building from scratch. As he placed a percussion cap on the nipple, he made sure he remembered to aim low if a good buck came along. He had only had time to shoot the gun a few times the day before and it shot high. Darkness had interrupted his practice session, preventing him from getting the sights fine-tuned. Aiming low would be easy to remember. For now, the south wind was too good to pass up since it was ideal for this prime funnel location. Yes, fixing the sights on the frontloader was a matter he would take care of later.

As the dawn eerily illuminated the hardwoods, Mellencamp felt confident. Not every whitetail hunter would have. In the past few days of hunting Mellencamp had seen only a fork-horn buck and a doe. He was a persistent hunter, though, and his living room walls contained an impressive display of trophy whitetails that had all fallen to his arrows. Interestingly, until this morning, he had not hunted with a firearm for many years.

The morning grew brighter, birds became active and a few squirrels darted about. No deer, however, used the funnel. The mid-morning hours passed and the noon hour finally rolled around. Still no deer. This didn't concern Mellencamp to any degree since several of his top deer had been tagged at midday. At 12:30 p.m. deer, as they can magically do, materialized in the timber. There were two doe, two yearling bucks, and an absolute monster. Cautiously they moved through the funnel. When the giant whitetail was broadside, Mellencamp, one of the finest shots I have ever known, raised his gun, lined the sights up, and as instinct would have any expert shot do, placed the sights on the great buck's kill zone. He squeezed the trigger.

THE PERFECT FUNNEL

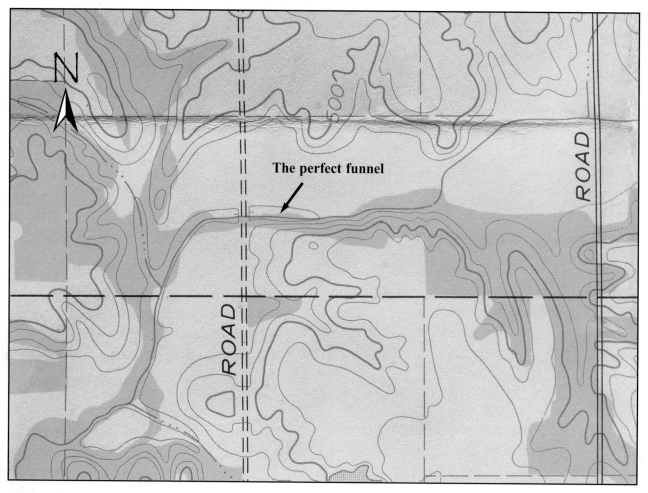

The perfect funnel

A lot of what made Mellencamp's hunt a success had to do with the fact that he had the buck in a perfect funnel. If there is one absolute about topography it is this: If you can find a perfect funnel, figure out a way to hunt it. The perfect funnel brings deer to you.

Looking at **Illustration 3.1** you will find a section of a topographic map where there is a narrow strip of timber connecting two larger tracts of woods. You should quickly recognize the advantage to hunting in this position. Simply put, any deer that is in the large section of forest to the west of the funnel will use the perfect funnel to get to the large forested tract to the east. And vice versa for a deer in timber east of the funnel.

In this layout, a north wind would allow you to walk across a field, probably harvested, from the south, take a stand on the south side of the narrow funnel, and remain undetected all day. A north wind, northwest wind, and northeast wind would all work perfectly to your advantage. In this particular setup, a near 180-degree range of wind directions could be used from the north. And as you can see, in this perfect funnel if you came in from the north, a variety of wind directions

from the south would also put the odds in your favor. Hunting on south winds, your effective wind usage in this funnel would also be very near to 180 degrees. When it comes to using the wind, it doesn't get much better than this.

Illustration 3.2 shows how the deer trails in the perfect funnel on level ground might look. It also shows the hunter's approach to stand, his position, and the wind direction. I have shown the field on the west side of the funnel to be a plowed field. This is the most perfect layout you will ever come across, for even after you leave the hunting area in the evening, deer will have no reason to venture out in the plowed field during the night. Not only will they not be able to detect you while you are on stand, they will never know you were ever there. This means you could hunt the stand frequently without ever creating alarm among the herd.

This is important, because your first hunt is always the most productive if you are pursuing a trophy whitetail. From the first hunt on, your odds go down. After the first hunt, he knows you're there—or that you've been there. That's what makes hunting big bucks such an interesting game.

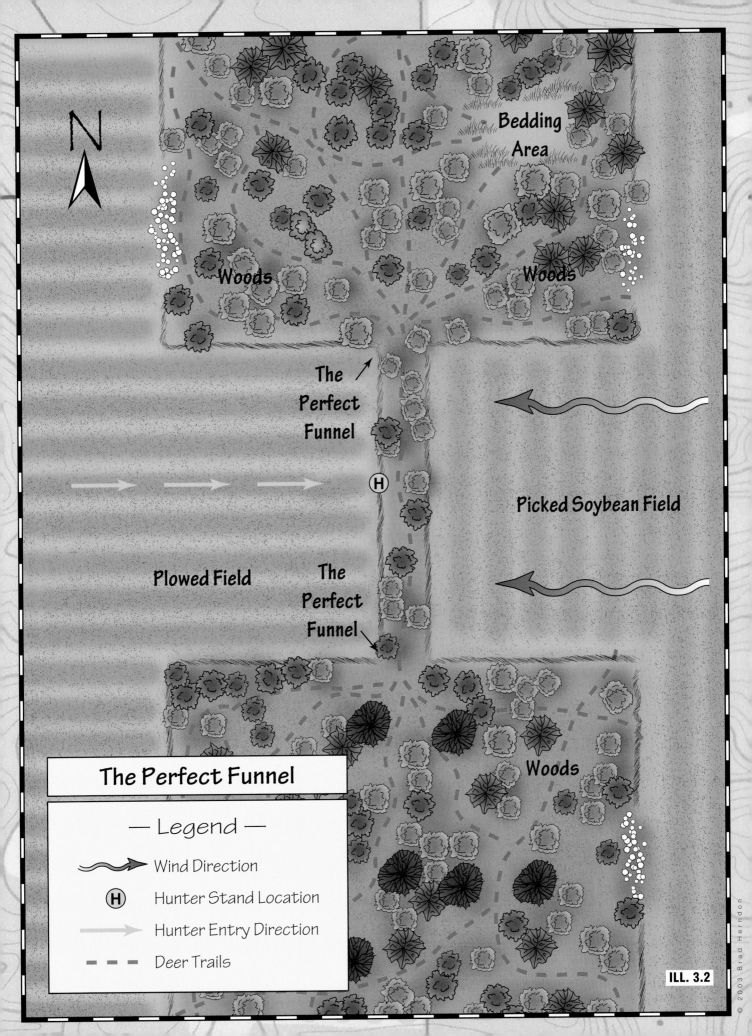

Bedding Area

Woods

Woods

The Perfect Funnel

Picked Soybean Field

H

Plowed Field

The Perfect Funnel

Woods

The Perfect Funnel

— Legend —

Wind Direction

H Hunter Stand Location

Hunter Entry Direction

Deer Trails

ILL. 3.2

© 2003 Brad Herndon

You can't beat a funnel if you want to video your hunts. The setup shown is perfect for over-the-shoulder photography, with the back stand being higher than the front stand.

Instantly the woods was filled with blackpowder smoke. Deer darted in varying directions. When the smoke cleared, Mellencamp could see the tremendous buck—still standing. Yes, he had forgotten to aim low. Who knows why, but the whitetail continued to stand there. Possibly it was because the deer had survived 5-1/2 years of hunting pressure and poaching by not acting in a hasty manner. Maybe he sensed since there was only one shot, it had been directed at another deer nearby. Maybe it was divine intervention. Whatever the reason, the great deer stood still, alert and searching.

Slowly, methodically, Mellencamp began his reloading procedure. As he did so, he doubted if he would ever get another shot off. His powder, patches, roundballs and caps were all in different places, some of them in his pant's pockets under his coveralls. Unbelievably, over a few minutes Mellencamp was able to reload the smokepole. The trophy whitetail, while looking carefully around during this time, had never moved his feet.

Mellencamp made sure to aim plenty low, quickly cocked the gun and fired. The giant buck collapsed. It was every bit as big as it looked, too. The 18-point bruiser grossed over 183 inches, with net typical score being only 159 1/8 inches thanks to numerous deductions, both from mismatched asymmetry and sticker points.

I love to hear Jay Mellencamp tell about this hunt because it is, to me, one of the most amazing kills on a mature deer I have ever heard. He was so cool in his reloading, never hurrying any movement despite that this brute buck was nearby and on full alert. I suspect many deer hunters, including me, would have rushed something and the buck would have blown out of there.

Of course there are several other aspects of this hunt which are fascinating as well. These include the topography in which he was hunting, his approach, the wind direction, and the time of day he finally experienced action. Let's see what enabled Mellencamp to make this successful hunt.

What To Look For

The perfect funnel has other names. Choke point, deer travel corridor, bottleneck, and narrows (Jay Mellencamp's name for them) are but a few. Regardless of what they are called they all serve the same purpose — bringing deer through a narrow piece of terrain that will give an observant hunter a close-range shot.

These funnels may be found in a variety of places, encompassing a vast array of terrain types. The topographical map will allow you to uncover most of them, while the aerial map will show them, but to a lesser degree. In this chapter I'll cover several of the ones on flat land and a few on hilly land, where possible. Other chapters will cover the hills to a much greater degree.

If you live on flat land such as might be found in portions of Illinois, Iowa, Ohio, Indiana and several other states, finding these perfect funnels is going to be fairly easy when using a map. First of all, look for the terrain configurations I have illustrated in this chapter. The funnel may be a strip of timber in flat farm country connecting two woodlots or larger tracts of timber. It may also be a strip of trees alongside a river or stream which serves as a connecting link between timbered sections of land. Don't overlook any feature of land or water.

For example, I know of one great funnel that is the top of a dam bank between two lowland hills. It's a quick route for whitetails to use when traveling from one hill to the other. A few miles from my home there's a field where I can see a wooden ground blind sitting about 100 yards away from a state highway bridge I cross. There is a National Wildlife Refuge on one side of this bridge,

Today's youngsters are very smart and will quickly pick up on how to read a topographical map when assisted by an adult.

private land on the other side. Deer coming out of the refuge go underneath the bridge alongside the river, then go downstream to other woodlots.

The hunter leaves this wooden ground blind up year round so the deer are used to it. When firearms season comes in, someone can drop him off at the bridge when the wind is best and he can slip across the field to the blind. Deer have no idea what's going on until it's too late.

Swamps are always worth looking at as well, since their outer edges can "bulge" out near a field or pasture and will create a really neat choke point. A unique feature about this type of funnel is that you have options regarding your entry to the stand. You can come in through a field with one wind direction and be in nice position. Another option on a different wind is found by making an approach by water to your stand, using a canoe, boat, or possibly even chest waders. Of course the previously mentioned wooded funnels alongside streams and rivers also afford a water approach to stand for deer hunters.

Getting into and out of your stand site without deer knowing you have ever been there is what you're after. At times a creek can be used as a means of pulling this off.

By hunting shed antlers in the off-season, much can be learned about your hunting terrain. By marking on a map the locations where shed antlers are found, patterns of deer movement can often be discovered.

Figuring Out Fencerows

Fencerows can be fantastic hunting locations and should be given careful consideration. Although I devote an entire chapter to fencerows I'm also mentioning them at this time because some of them certainly fall in the perfect funnel category. Unless they are fairly wide, fencerows will be designated as dashed red lines on topographical maps, so in most cases it will be impossible to determine what type of habitat they contain. Aerial maps do a better job of interpreting fencerows since they show the brush or trees in a fencerow. Obtain the most recent aerial maps you can, since landowners frequently clear fencerows.

In some areas of the nation, clean farming practices are not as prevalent as in other regions. The extreme southern part of Illinois comes to my mind. Here you can find fencerows wide enough, and with enough brush, for deer to travel within their interior. These fencerows serve as links between various tracts of timber. They are, as one might think, super places to ambush a bruiser buck,

Mature bucks like this escape hunters every year. Figure out how they use the terrain to evade hunters and you may very well put your tag on him next hunting season.

especially since Illinois is one of the top trophy-producing states in our country. More often than not, though, fencerows will not be wide enough to allow deer to move within the interior. Instead the whitetails will hold tight to, and travel parallel with the fencerow when traveling through a region. My good friend Henry Reynolds can attest to this.

One year, Henry decided to scout a hilly region he was somewhat familiar with. He wasn't very optimistic since one full week of firearms season had already passed by, and he knew the location he was studying was like a war zone on opening day. Still, since Reynolds is a careful hunter, he inched into the area very slowly, carefully glassing the region for deer movement. Moving into a small, flat, ridge-top farming area, he noticed it was a hub on top where four gullies headed up. At the top of each gully, where they joined the fields, a fencerow started, each one stretching across the fields to the gully on the opposite side. These two fencerows formed an X where

When this picture was taken in 1989, Cullen Stahl—The Midday Master—had already taken several dandy bucks during the midday hours. In the ensuing years, he's taken many more outstanding whitetails during this time period.

they crossed in the middle of the fields.

Reynolds thought, "There can't be any big bucks left here because of the hunting pressure." Just then, he noticed movement near one of the fencerows. Kneeling down, he raised his binoculars and was amazed to see a great buck. There wasn't anything he could do at this point since the wind was wrong and he was across an open field from the bruiser. Continuing his watch, my friend shook with excitement as he watched six different mature whitetails use the fencerow. Although he had no idea how that many great deer survived in the region, Reynolds did know he would be back when a northwest wind was blowing. That was the only wind direction he could use to outsmart these surviving brutes.

Do bucks bed down because of excess hunting pressure, or because they are tired? Hunting at midday may change your mind regarding this answer.

It took three days of waiting for the wind to be right. Even then Reynolds decided to slip into the fencerow right after daylight, since he wanted to be extra careful. Easing along, he drew within 100 yards of the fencerow and saw movement! A huge buck, larger than any of the others he had previously seen, was dogging a doe. Quickly, my buddy snuggled his shotgun to his shoulder, waiting for an opportunity to shoot. Just then the doe hesitated, causing the buck to stop. The report pierced the still morning and the 160-class buck bolted away. A miss.

Yes, not every hunt ends successfully. Nevertheless, something positive came from this hunt since both my friend and I learned even more about fencerows and how deer use them. He has been successful in this fencerow region since then, although he hasn't yet taken a monster there. As you may have guessed by now, the terrain configurations made the deer trails in each gully funnel up to the top, then the fencerows served as covered travel corridors for the deer to go from one side to the other.

Reynold's fencerow hunt wasn't the perfect hunt because of the configuration of the terrain and the way the fencerows crossed. Still, it's a good example of what to look for. There are a few perfect funnels formed when deer follow some of these little-noticed fencerows and you should be aware of how strategic they can be.

If a road is nearby, deer will use the backsides of these fencerows when traveling about. They may favor either side of the fencerow in the absence of houses and roads. If no trees are present for tree stand use, ground blinds will work well when hunting fencerows. Both natural blinds and commercial ground blinds will do the job. They must, however, be in place well before season since it takes a while for deer to get used to them.

Timing The Perfect Funnel

You may be surprised as you read this book to find many bucks will be killed between the hours of 11:00 a.m. and 1:00 p.m. This is not unusual, although many

MY FAVORITE STAND

I hunt hilly land more than I do flat land, but my favorite stand site is found on flat land where the wind is easy to use. I like to locate two large tracts of woods connected by a narrow tract of timber no more than 100 yards wide. If each woods contains a doe bedding area, so much the better. I prefer this funnel to lay in an east/west direction so I can use any type of north or south wind to hunt the pinch point.

Ideally a field or pasture will be found on both sides of this narrow strip of connecting timber, and this enables me to make a perfect entry to my stand site. In this setup, mature books will travel from one large section of woods to the other when out searching for doe in heat, and when they do they will walk right past my stand. The tail end of the rut is great for this location, too.

Whether it's bow or firearm season, this stand location can't be beat for hunting older whitetail bucks.

Henry Reynolds

Having fruit or high-energy snacks along will help you stay on stand through the midday period. You might be surprised what shows up when the sun is at its zenith!

Believe it or not, the best time for an archer to take a Pope & Young buck is during the midday period, from 11:00 a.m. until 2:00 p.m.!

whitetail hunters might think so. Another great friend of mine, Cullen Stahl, can attest to the advantages of midday hunting. In fact, I call him The Midday Master.

November 10, 1978 was the date of the first midday kill for Stahl. This buck was a big-bodied 11-point. Interestingly, at the time of this kill a farmer was fall plowing nearby and the farmer's young son was sitting at the edge of Stahl's wood singing songs as he watched his dad work. Since that time Stahl has killed several more trophy whitetails at midday, with the majority falling to his arrow or bullet between noon and 1:00 p.m.

"Most old bucks spend the nights during the rut searching for does," Stahl noted. "They burn up a tremendous amount of energy during the night on their rounds and by daybreak most of them are quite tired. Because of this I believe many of them bed down for a few hours each morning. By 10:30 a.m. or a little later they are somewhat rested up. They then get up, stretch a little, and cautiously start moving. At this time they will check out the doe bedding areas, often until 1:00 p.m. or later, then they will bed down again.

"Most hunters think mature bucks bed down because of hunting pressure — and some do — and then get up and move around during midday because the hunters are gone," Stahl said. "This is a nice romantic theory, but not one I believe to be true to any great degree. More big bucks aren't killed during the midday period for the simple reason not many hunters are still on stand then."

What The Statistics Say

The Pope & Young records show archers harvest 52 percent of Pope & Young bucks between 4 p.m. and sunset. Another 17 percent of book entries are tagged between sunrise and 8:00 a.m. The three-hour time period from 8:00 a.m. until 11:00 a.m. accounts for 19 percent of the entries, while the 2:00 p.m. until 4:00 p.m. time frame produces 9 percent of the entries. Add these figures up and it tallies a full 97 percent of all entries. This is impressive.

Meanwhile, poor old Bowhunter Joe, who is torturing himself by staying on stand between the hours of 11:00 a.m. until 2:00 p.m. accounts for only 3 percent of the total. If we study these figures without taking any other factor into consideration it seems like a no-brainer: We should spend most of our time hunting in the evening, and if not then, certainly sunrise until 10:00 a.m. or so should be our choice. This type of hunting leaves us plenty of time to get out of the woods in the morning, eat, nap, chop a little wood, and still get back for that electrifying evening hunt.

But there is far more than meets the eye regarding these statistics.

For instance, the number of hunters afield for each time period must be factored in to enable us to get a success ratio. Without question evening is a fantastic time for an archer to taste success on a whitetail scoring over 125. This is true because the hunter can, if he's careful, make his way to the stand without being detected by the deer. If he's got the wind in his favor, he then can simply wait until the deer move late in the evening and bingo, he's got a book buck. It works.

But if it takes 60 percent of the total man-hours of bow hunting to take 52 percent of the book entries, does the evening hunt give you the highest odds of taking a Pope & Young buck? I can answer this question. It doesn't. Let's go back to poor old Bowhunter Joe, who by now is starving in his tree at high noon.

Bowhunter Joe's hours on stand between 11:00 a.m. and 2:00 p.m. constitute only 1 percent of the total number of hours invested in bow hunting each year. This means the midday hunter, who is investing just 1 percent of the total bow hunting hours, is tagging a full 3 percent

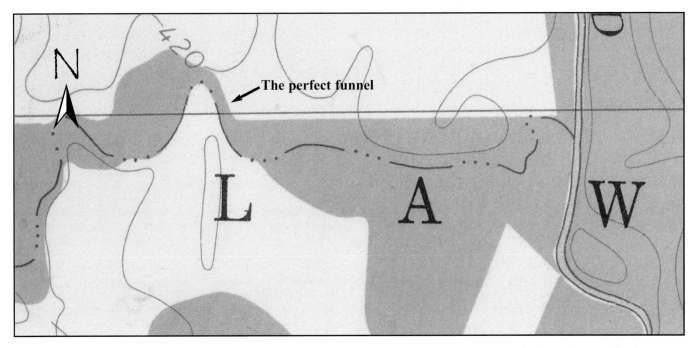

A topo map will quickly reveal this hot funnel location. A setup like this is a perfect location in which to take a trophy during the midday period when he's out searching for hot does.

of the book entries! Believe it or not, this is the highest success rate of any hunter afield, at any time of the day. As my friend Cullen Stahl said, few high scoring trophy whitetails are taken during the midday period for the simple fact very few hunters are still in the woods at that time.

I have added up all of the mature bucks Carol and I, plus all of our trophy-hunting friends, have taken throughout the past 20 years and close to 50 percent of them were taken between the hours of 10:30 a.m. and 1:00 p.m. And listen to what my longtime friend David Blanton, producer of Realtree's Popular *Monster Bucks* video series has to say.

"If someone told me 11 years ago that I would be expected to sit out on the stand from before daylight until after dark on certain hunts, I would have told them, 'Okay, but it sure will be a waste of time.' And how wrong I would have been! Probably the most important thing I've learned in 10 years of producing *Monster Bucks* videos is just how much mature bucks move outside of the traditional early and late windows, especially around the pre-rut and rut phases. As a matter of fact, when I go to Canada, I don't get really focused until the late morning because we see more big bucks between 11:00 a.m. and 2:00 p.m. than any other period of the day."

Yes, the midday period can be hot during the rut and post rut. My favorite time to hunt is at the tail end of the rut when the buster boys are out searching for the few remaining does in heat. And although I believe age and personalities have some influence on how easy it is for

hunters to remain on stand for long hours, confidence is the ultimate key to being successful at the midday game. This is not to say you should quit hunting early and late; they are great times to be afield. I'm just saying that you should give the midday period a try for a few days each year.

Typically Carol and I hunt until 1:00 p.m., take a break, and then get back on a stand about 3:30 in the evening if we are on a full-day hunt. Regarding weather conditions, all of us in southern Indiana who chase big whitetails have found a cool, crisp sunny morning, with temperatures rising into the 50s later in the day to be the best weather conditions for midday deer movement.

Dr. James C. Kroll, one of the most respected deer biologists in the nation, concurred with our views in his book *Producing and Harvesting White-tailed Deer*.

"Deer movements are influenced by relative humidity as well," Kroll noted. "Several studies have shown that deer are more active on days with low relative humidity. For a generalized model, I have found that deer prefer days with cold to moderate temperatures, little wind, less than 50 percent cloud cover and no more than 60 to 70 percent relative humidity. What I am describing here is a fine fall day! The kind of day that you yourself prefer to move around in; after all, you too are an animal."

So while finding perfect funnels will be instrumental in your deer hunting, so will using the wind wisely. And so will knowing when to hunt and how long to hunt. Jay Mellencamp is successful because he puts all of the parts of the puzzle together so very well. You can do the same.

Chapter 4

The Hilltop Field Funnel

After leasing more than 300 acres of rolling hills, Henry Reynolds spent considerable time painstakingly studying the hilly region. The terrain features and deer trails in one long hollow on the property especially interested him. A field bordered the long hollow on the south side. The hillside of the hollow adjacent to this field contained numerous deer trails running parallel to the field. Halfway down the hollow's length, a small stream forked from the main stream and cut its way up to the field's edge. The sides of this small stream were steep and hard to walk. Because of this, all of the deer trails on the hillside, running parallel to the field's edge angled up toward the top of this small stream. Eventually they all converged at the top of the stream near the field, then dispersed once more, many of them snaking back down the hillside.

Henry Reynolds took this fine 9-point buck by hunting a hilltop field funnel in southern Indiana.

This feature, one Reynolds recognized as a hilltop field funnel, looked to be a good place to install one of his tree stands. One November morning when the rut had kicked in, Reynolds caught the north wind he needed. In the woods way earlier than most hunters ever get there, Reynolds climbed to his elevated platform. He had pop, chips and other snacks to sustain him for several hours. He was ready.

The glow of a crisp, clear morning lit up the forest floor below him. Reynolds could see the torn up trails the deer had been using, all coming together just north of him. He watched them intently. At the same time, he also watched the field behind him. The field bordering the hilltop field funnel actually curved back down to the funnel from above, then back up. This meant the inset of the field lay directly

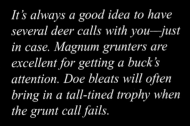

It's always a good idea to have several deer calls with you—just in case. Magnum grunters are excellent for getting a buck's attention. Doe bleats will often bring in a tall-tined trophy when the grunt call fails.

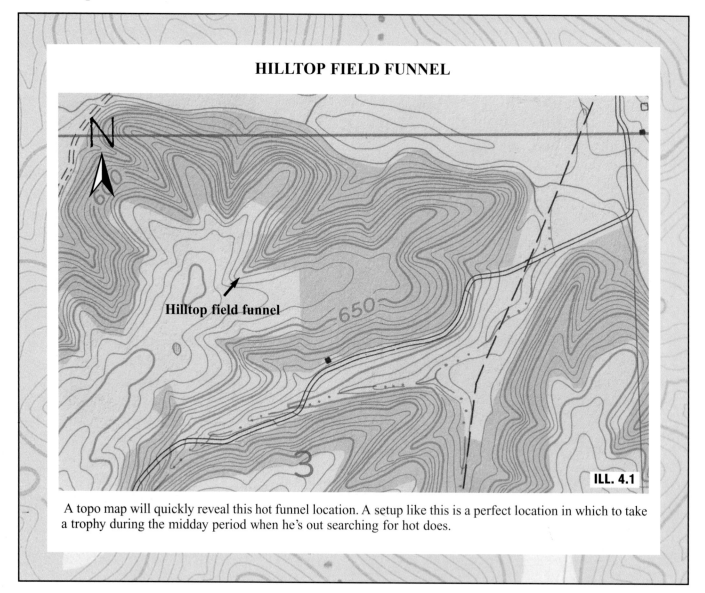

HILLTOP FIELD FUNNEL

ILL. 4.1

A topo map will quickly reveal this hot funnel location. A setup like this is a perfect location in which to take a trophy during the midday period when he's out searching for hot does.

behind Reynolds, but perhaps off to each side of him 100 yards or so, the hardwoods actually ran behind him. Most likely any deer traveling through the hilltop field funnel area would take the deer trail directly in front of him. But Reynolds knew a buck, in his hurry to save a few seconds of travel, might pop out of the timber before it got to the funnel and cross the short section of field behind him.

A little after 10:00 a.m. Reynolds was taking in some liquid and reaching for a potato chip when he noticed movement in the field behind him and to the east. Yes, a buck had popped out of the timber and was taking the unlikely shortcut behind him. A well-placed 12-gauge slug put the trophy on the ground. It turned out to be a 9-point, 4-1/2-year-old buck. The gross score was in the 140s; net was 137 inches. It was a dandy whitetail.

Topo Maps Will Tell All

A hilltop field funnel, when hunted with the wind in your favor, will enable you to tag deer of various ages. Does, fawns, young bucks, and even your hunting territory's top-end trophies will filter through this outstanding deer travel corridor. If you hunt smart, filling your tag in this location on younger deer should be easy, in both bow and firearms seasons. This is true because the hilltop field funnel offers you a close-range shot. It goes without saying older bucks won't be so easy, simply because they are smarter and there aren't nearly as many of them in most deer herds.

The good news about this type of funnel is that it is easy to identify by using a topographical map. In **Illustration 4.1** a section of a topo map is shown where a hilltop field funnel is located. The stream coming from

It's daybreak and you're just beginning a hunt in the hilly area of another state you know nothing about. Without a topographical map, it will take you days of walking to uncover the best hunting places. With a topo map, you'll know the hottest funnels to hunt before you ever leave home.

the valley below has steep hillsides on each side of it. We all know a whitetail could rip down and up these steep hillsides if they so desired; yet it's a rare case when they do. Instead, as the deer use trails lower on the hillsides, they will naturally take the path of least resistance. This means they will generally follow along beside the stream as it makes its way toward the top of the hill.

If a field or pasture is located at the top of the hill where the creek peters out, all of the deer trails on the side of the hill, plus any at the top of the hill, will all come together at this point. This type of spot is a favorite location for many hunters for a number of reasons.

First of all, these funnels, as mentioned, are easy to find in a hilly region if the hunter uses a topo map. Secondly, when a field or pasture is located at the top of the hill, this gives the deer hunter a perfect access to his stand site. Thirdly, because hilltop field funnels are located at or near the highest elevations of the hills, the wind stays consistent on most days. Finally, the position of the choke point allows a wide degree of wind directions to be effectively used by the hunter.

Late muzzleloader seasons are productive for many hunters who are willing to endure the brutal late-winter weather. Bottlenecks near high-energy food sources are high-odds stand sites.

Using The Wind

Illustration 4.2 shows what a typical hilltop field funnel looks like. In this drawing, the deer trails are shown so you can understand the general flow of deer movement in such a location. Also shown is the most favorable wind for a hunter to use in this specific configuration, and his stand position is noted along with how he made his entry to stand. The wind, as long as it is from a southerly direction of some sort, will allow the hunter to remain on stand as long as he desires without being noticed by any deer. The effective wind usage approaches 180 degrees, about as good as it gets. But not quite.

On Henry Reynolds hunt, he was sitting in a stand where the field curved to each side of him and back. This meant his safe wind usage may have been only about 90 degrees or so. This was why he was using a wind coming directly from the north. Some hilltop field funnels I hunt have the field curving away from my stand site. This affords me the opportunity of using winds approaching a 270 degree arc around me.

Hilltop field funnels may or may not have rubs and scrapes near them. What they will have, quite often, are heavily used, eye-catching deer trails etched in the soil before you. This type of deer sign may tempt you to hunt the funnel when the wind is less than perfect. For instance, let's assume you have a hilltop field funnel perfect for a west wind. You get up one morning, just knowing this is the day Old Megahorns is going to slide through this location. You groan when you learn the wind direction is from the east.

Not a problem. You decide to cross the field to stand like you always do. Then, instead of putting your tree stand between the funnel trail and the field, you cross the trail and place your stand on the west, or downwind side of the deer trail coming through the hilltop field funnel. Problem solved. Or so you think.

Actually, you've just made a big mistake, especially if you are trying to outsmart a trophy buck. Look at **Illustration 4.2** again. If you change the wind direction to the north in this drawing and hunt on the other (south) side of the trail, the deer coming up each side of the stream behind the stand will smell you from a great distance if the wind is off a little to one side, such as northeast or northwest. They will slip out of there, probably before you even notice them. They have smelled you and they know your ambush spot. By doing this you have lowered your chances of success greatly.

I mention this because we have a hilltop field funnel that is tempting to hunt this way. It's in a wide open woods where I can see a deer coming for at least 200

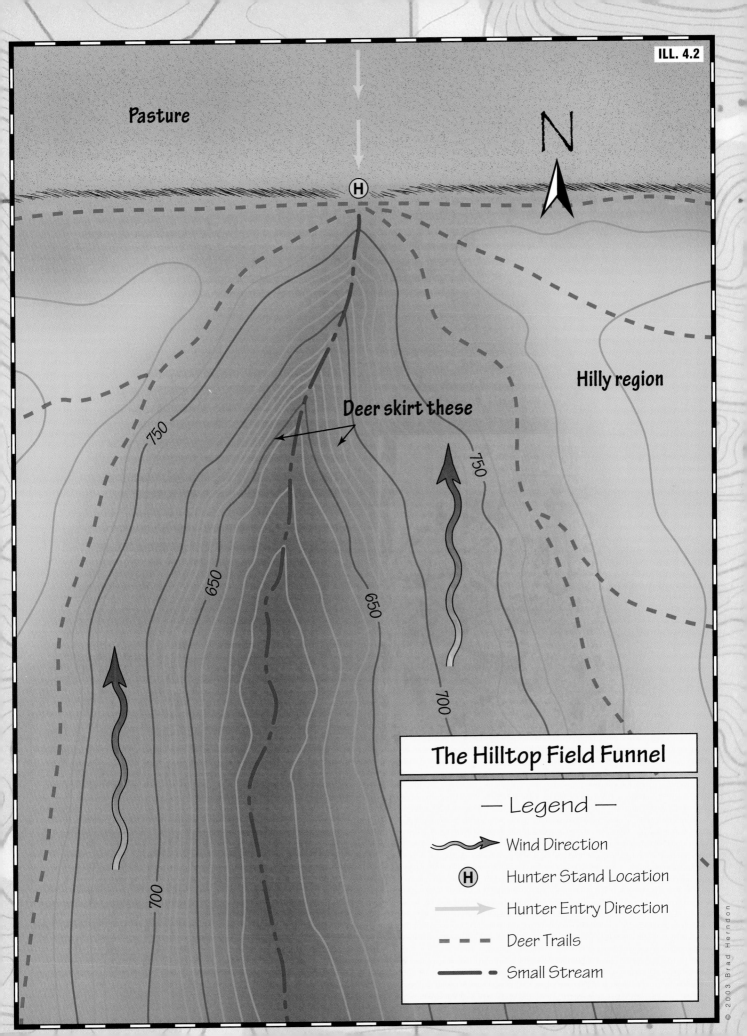

ILL. 4.2

Pasture

N

Hilly region

Deer skirt these

750

750

650

650

700

700

The Hilltop Field Funnel

— Legend —

Wind Direction

(H) Hunter Stand Location

Hunter Entry Direction

Deer Trails

Small Stream

Live to hunt another day. Regardless of how high or low you hunt, always use a safety belt or harness when hunting from a tree stand.

yards. Many times I've caught movement far below me alongside the stream leading up to my stand location. I then am able to watch as this deer comes slowly up the trail, finally turns into the funnel before me, and then waltzes by. Often I've considered what would happen if I tried hunting on the other side of the trail with an opposite wind direction. My answer every time is that such a hunt would be a disaster.

For this reason, hunt hilltop field funnels only when conditions are almost perfect. I can't stress enough how important it is to have a number of terrain traps scattered around. Have enough so any wind direction the day may bring will still be usable in some of your funnel ambush points.

Before looking further into the hills, I would like to add some input into tree stand height. As I write this I'm 59 years old. By the grace of God, I'm still in excellent health and able to trudge up and down hills as much as I want to. So is Carol. I suppose we could still get as high in a tree as we wanted to, yet every time I look down from my tree stand, I can understand the old saying, "The farther you fall, the harder you hit." Most of the tree stands we put up for Carol are about 13 feet high. Some of these we leave up year-round and I hunt out of them as well. If I'm hunting new regions and putting up my own stand each time, my stand height will fall in the 14- or 15-foot range.

We've never hunted very high, still don't, and hardly ever get noticed by deer passing our stand, even though we are oftentimes within 15 yards of them. This lack of notice occurs, I believe, because we use the wind very well, therefore deer don't smell us. Also, when we watch for deer, we are painfully careful about not making any sudden movements. Too many hunters alert whitetails to their presence by cranking their head back and forth in a jerking, rapid movement. Slow is the word, back and forth, hour after hour. We also wear camouflage that blends in well to the habitat we are hunting. It doesn't hurt any, either, that we are relatively small in stature.

Henry Reynolds, and a few other friends, hunt nosebleed high. It works for them. Basically, each hunter has to choose the height he feels comfortable with. This height will be determined by fear of height, size of trees, and a few other factors. I don't think you have to hunt high in order to be successful. This being said, there are a few times when you need to get up in the air more. A devil's backbone saddle comes to mind. Narrow in width, it may have hillsides sharply dropping off on each side of it. Getting 15 yards off to the side of this saddle and 15 feet up in a tree may put you only 7 or 8 feet high. In this case you may need to get 22 or

Only you can determine what stand to use, and what height you're comfortable with using. Ladder stands are safe, come in various heights, and deer pay no attention to them.

more feet up the tree.

Whether you hunt high or low, hunting smart in terrain traps will enable you to see more deer.

Bow hunters take some outstanding bucks from saddles. Saddles are good because they funnel whitetails down to a narrow travel corridor that is perfect for the archer and firearm hunter alike.

Chapter 5

Shooting From The Saddle

I'll admit it. I'm a ridge-running hillbilly from southern Indiana, and proud of it. I had the good fortune to grow up in Starve Hollow, a beautiful little valley separating two small ranges of hard-wood hills. My childhood was enjoyable because I got to explore the hills near my home and poke into all the fascinating aspects of nature. I came across copper-heads and rattlesnakes, swung on grapevines on the hill-sides, and in the fall spent every minute I could hunting squirrels. Deer hunting, however, was not an option when I was young, since whitetails were as scarce as hen's teeth where I lived.

When I reached adulthood, things had changed. The bottom lands held deer and this is where I started hunting in 1968. The hill deer came later. By 1985 whitetails were prevalent enough near my home, which is about 4 miles away from where I was raised, to start hunting them. This was the beginning of my serious study of hilly terrain, and how deer moved about within these regions. By 1987, whitetail sign was increasing in Starve Hollow near The Home Place (that's what the sign said in front of mom and dad's house) to the point that I started seri-ously hunting that section of the hills since it brought back so many wonderful memories.

On Nov. 12, 1987 I arrived at The Home Place well before daylight and parked in the gravel driveway. It brought back memories of pushing old rattletrap Fords down the driveway in attempts to start them on cold mornings. Gathering up my bow, tree stand and other

Riding the saddle is productive hunting because the low spot in a ridgeline funnels deer like this right to you.

Saddles can be visible in ridgelines located close to roads. The dip in the ridgeline in the left side of this picture is the high saddle where the author got a crack at The Hill Buck back in 1987.

gear, I slipped across the little creek behind the house, walked past the old cellar house and was soon beginning the strenuous climb up the steep hickory grove hill. After a laborious climb, I walked east to where two ridgetops met, hung a right and traveled south about 1/4-mile. I found the saddle, a low spot in the ridgeline, where I intended to spend the day. Soon I had my stand positioned to take advantage of the 5 to 15 mph southwest wind predicted for the day.

Within minutes a beautiful sunrise illuminated the Wegan Church to my east. All was right with the world. As I watched the deer trails before me, I once more marveled at the one coming from the southeast. It actually snaked about 1-1/2 miles from some lowland farm fields below, came almost to the center of the saddle where it then crossed the ridge and looped back to the southwest to a bedding area. By climbing up the steep hill and dropping over it the deer could have saved themselves a half mile of walking to get to the bedding area. But like humans, whitetails are lazy and will take the easiest walking route, even if it's longer. The saddle was easier.

Another trail came into the saddle from the northwest. Deer coming from this direction came through the saddle, then branched off on one fork of the looping trail. There was no deer trail running the length of the ridge, and only a faint trail came into the saddle from the northeast. The trail layout had determined my approach to stand. Now if The Hill Buck, a legendary whitetail I knew about, would only show up the day would be complete.

Motivation From The Midday Master

At 8:00 a.m. I noticed a doe coming from the southeast. Once she reached the saddle, instead of looping southwest she walked into the saddle and eventually moved down the trail going northwest. Movement on this same trail at 10:30 a.m. revealed a young-looking 6-point buck coming my way. After he came through the

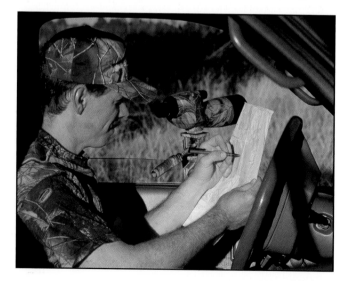

By using a spotting scope during the summer months, you can discover some real monster bucks. Once you've located trophies, study your topographical maps to uncover any terrain funnels within their home range. Saddles always are great places to ambush brute bucks.

saddle, he split down the deer trail to the southeast. Both of these deer had walked within 12 yards of me. Where was The Hill Buck?

I knew when it was high noon as the distinctive tone of the whistle at the paper mill in Brownstown, 6 miles away, reached my ears. Looking down at my watch to confirm the time, I said, "Here we go, Cullen."

As I've noted elsewhere, my good friend Cullen Stahl has tagged a truckload of huge deer between noon and 1:00 p.m. I call him The Midday Master, and it was his example that inspired me and motivated me to hang tough on the serene ridgetop.

The early morning temperature of 44 degrees had risen into the 60s. I knew the time of year and these weather conditions were ideal for giant buck movement. I wasn't giving up. As the sun made its slow arc over the ridgetop I heard a loud crashing to the west, on the other side of the saddle. Looking quickly at my watch, I noted the time. 12:52 p.m. The crashing got louder and louder. It had to be a deer, although surprisingly to me it wasn't coming up the hill on any deer trail. Instead it was barging through an entanglement of green briers. Just in case it was a mature buck, I placed my release on the bow string.

Within a few seconds a huge-bodied deer appeared at the edge of the saddle. It was the most memorable experience of my deer hunting career. Standing there, strands of greenbrier draping from his antlers, was The Hill Buck. He was tremendously wide and massive, with 12 bulky points projecting toward the heavens. He looked left, then right. Everything told me he would come my way.

I was at full draw as he briskly walked my way. When he was perhaps 30 yards away, he pulled the unexpected. Instead of coming through the saddle, he dropped over the side of the hill behind, but toward, me. Turning completely in my tree stand, I watched as he angled toward me—25 yards, 20 yards, 15 yards. He stopped, stiff as a statue. He had crossed my entry trail from earlier in the morning and knew something was wrong. Even though I didn't like the angle he was facing, I knew the jig was up. It was now or never. Placing the sight pin a safe distance behind his shoulder, I released the arrow.

The next few seconds were a blur. The great buck spun around and bounded to the northwest. Sickeningly I watched as he ran because a great length of my arrow was protruding from his shoulder, not the kill area. My shot had looked so good, the release had felt so clean, yet the dreaded shoulder shot was the result of my efforts. Looking back — and I have hundreds of times — I've often wondered if The Hill Buck jumped the string since he was alert, and this resulted in the bad hit. I'll never know what happened.

After waiting two hours I starting the tracking job, one I knew would have no end. Shortly I found my bro-

If you're an archer, remove any tree limbs that might interfere with your shot when a big whitetail comes along.

ken arrow shaft. As expected, the broadhead and a few inches of arrow had remained in the deer's shoulder. I suspected the deer would head to a thicket caused by a fire a few years earlier, and he did. I could find occasional drops of blood as I followed the trail almost 2 miles. He had bedded two times. Near dark I found one drop of blood at the edge of the thicket. The next morning I was back at the same place and by searching the thicket I found a large deer bed, a few drops of blood, and nothing more.

I was totally crushed by this series of events. Nevertheless, I was confident The Hill Buck was alive and well, sore and smarter. Would I ever see him again?

I did, in an unexpected way. The next year, several miles away, on a slick rain-soaked night, The Hill Buck made a bound across a highway while pursuing a doe. He had time to beat the approaching van, but when his hooves hit the glass-like pavement his feet went out from under him, causing him to fall in the middle of the road. The van did what no hunter had ever been able to do—it killed him.

Fortunately I heard about the accident and was able to see the deer I had hunted for so long. He was everything I expected him to be. He carried a 21-1/2-inch inside spread framed with 27-inch-long main beams. Antler mass was over 40 inches, with five of the circumferences being over 5 inches. The tine length, while good, was not outstanding. Gross typical score was 189-7/8 inches; net 182-7/8 inches. The great deer was most likely 6-1/2 years old. Despite looking rail-thin from his doe chasing endeavors, his large frame still weighed 202 pounds field-dressed.

This is The Hill Buck, another great deer that was never killed by a hunter. His gross typical score is 189 7/8 inches, net is 182 7/8 inches.

Surveillance cameras can provide you with a lot of fun. They can often surprise you by revealing a tremendous buck, one you have never seen before, is using your hunting area.

Low Deer Numbers, Good Success Rate

I shared this hunt so you might get a feel for hunting saddles in hilly regions, both from an emotional and hunting standpoint. Interestingly, this hunt took place on public land and was actually part of my pre-planning for the 1987 hunting season. In the past I had seen one set of sheds from The Hill Buck when he was 3-1/2 years old. When he was 4-1/2 years old, I received a report a farmer had found his matched set of sheds, but I was never able to track them down. In 1987 there were not many deer in the range of hills where I was hunting. This meant few does were there to be in heat at any one time. Therefore, The Hill Buck would most likely cover several square miles during the rut and tail end of the hunt in search of the few estrous does the region would contain. Knowing saddles were strategic corridors deer used, my strategy was to sit on stand in these locations in hopes The Hill Buck would come through.

As you just read, this was a long shot that nearly paid off. It did, I have to admit, take a great degree of determination to stay the course. To give you an idea why it was difficult from a confidence standpoint to hunt these saddles, consider the following numbers: In 1987 I made 22 deer hunts during bow and firearm seasons. My total sightings of deer from stand for the year was 38. My two best outings, were in December when I saw seven and four deer, respectively, on two different hunts. I had eight hunts, some of them long ones, when I saw no whitetails at all.

RECOGNIZING SADDLES

ILL. 5.1

Saddle

Pick up a topo map of a hilly region and start studying the terrain features it contains. Quite as you might expect, what you see will depend on how hilly the region is where you live. There will be similarities in what you see in all hilly regions, such as streams, roads, houses, ponds, and things of that nature. Elevations, however, can vary greatly. Mountainous regions will contain great heights. Low, rolling hills will not. Regardless of this, saddles can be found in all of these locations. Some will be grand in scale, others indiscreet. For simplicity sake, the illustrations I'll use will be the height of hills most often encountered when hunting in many states, particularly the Midwest.

Illustration 5.1 shows a section of a topographical map. Green designates the tract as being solid timber. In other words, it's a vast, hilly region, the type of terrain many deer hunters have trouble figuring out. Following the contour lines as they rise in elevation, you will see the tops of ridges. A saddle can be seen in this topo map. It is formed when the ridge length drops down in elevation, then goes back up. This forms a low spot in the ridgeline. This is the saddle.

The saddle, being the lowest location in the ridgeline, makes a perfect spot for whitetails to cross when going from one side of a hill to the other. If you are out wandering around in the hills, covering several miles per day, you will find yourself using saddles in a similar manner. You ease along a hillside, and it naturally funnels you to the saddle. On topo maps you will see there are varying heights of saddles. Some are high, containing very little drop in elevation. Others are medium in height, while a few

are what I call deep-gap saddles, containing a considerable drop in elevation.

Their width varies, too. Some may be narrow, perfect for the bow hunter. Others may be medium in width, and still others wide. The wide ones are easier for the firearm hunter to take advantage of.

Regardless of their height or width, most of the saddles you find will be great locations in which to place your stand. Even so, be aware that some will be better than others. If a ridgeline contains only one saddle, and there is 3,000 acres of woods on each side of it, you have found a dynamite location. Conversely, if a saddle has 1,000 acres of woods on one side of it and a shopping center on the other side, it may not be so hot. Ultimately, you have to determine how good a saddle is by spending time there during a few hunts.

Besides being the best deer funnel in the hills, a saddle is located up high. This means the wind generally stays the same throughout the day, allowing you to expertly use the wind directions to carry your scent away to the least likely place deer might appear. The only time the wind might mess with you in a saddle is when the saddle is nestled in a deep gap. Then you will have to carefully evaluate what wind direction will work best there.

When reading topo maps at home, you can lay a compass on the map and determine the best wind directions for the saddles you discover. If it is possible I like to scout in the post-season and actually stand in these saddles and hold my compass in my hand and see what winds I can use when hunting the location.

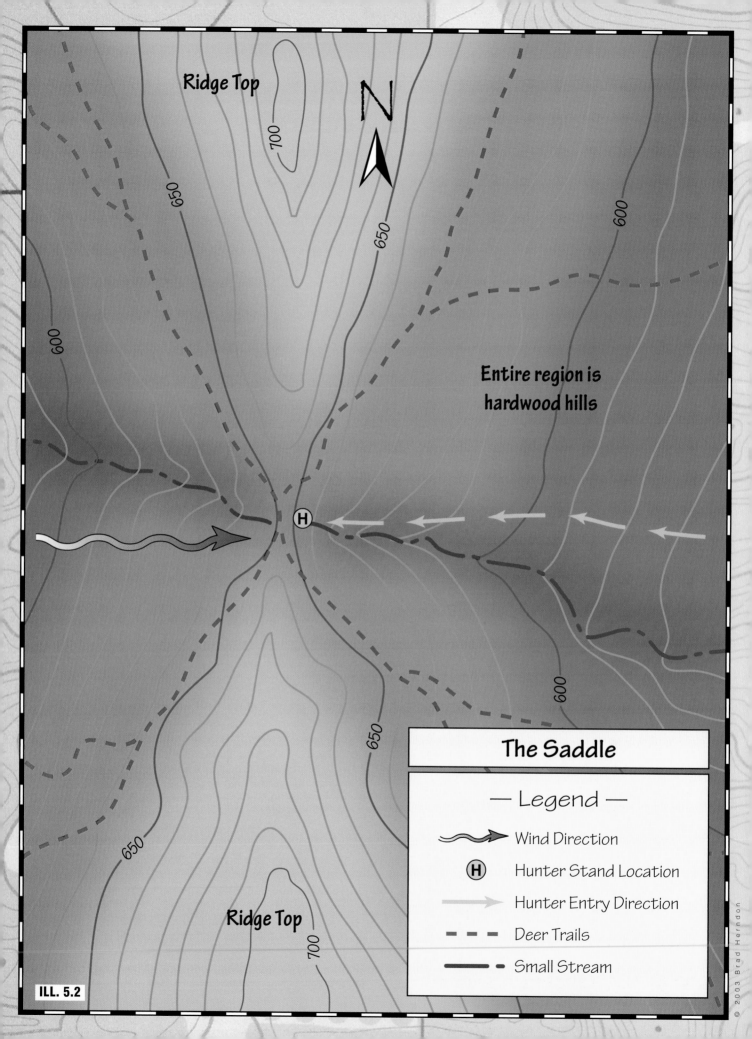

Ridge Top

700

650

600

650

600

N

Entire region is
hardwood hills

(H)

Ridge Top

600

650

650

700

The Saddle

— Legend —

Wind Direction

(H) Hunter Stand Location

Hunter Entry Direction

Deer Trails

Small Stream

ILL. 5.2

© 2003 Brad Herndon

If you know how to use a topo map and a compass, you can hunt out West and never get lost.

Despite these low numbers, Carol killed an 8-point, 4-1/2-year old buck that year that grossed in the 140s and netted 137 inches. It was taken in a saddle less than one mile from where I hunted. Two days after she filled her gun tag, I killed a 3-1/2-year old 8-point out of the same saddle where I had a crack at The Hill Buck. So we had great success hunting saddles in 1987 despite the low deer population.

Few areas of the country have low deer densities like this anymore. This means if you learn to recognize saddles in the hills when walking or studying topographical maps, and then put sound hunting principles into practice, you should have opportunities at shooting any deer you desire in the part of the country you hunt.

Getting In And Out

In **Illustration 5.2** I have drawn a saddle similar to most of the ones we hunt here in southern Indiana. I have shown the contour elevation lines, the general movement of the deer, the route the hunter took to the stand, wind direction, and so on. When deciding how to get to the saddle you are going to hunt, the layout of the deer trails in the terrain will determine what approach you make. Much of the time there will not be a deer trail running the length of the ridge. This will allow you to walk along the ridge

As this picture reveals, a saddle was instrumental in the author taking this fine buck from a public hunting area.

and then drop into your saddle placement. You cross only one deer trail this way. Make sure you cross the least-used trail and you will increase your odds of success.

If there is a deer trail on top of the ridge, or if it just isn't feasible to enter from that way, then the small stream leading up to the midsection of the saddle is a super entry way to a saddle stand site. Hunt with a wind perpendicular to the ridge and your scent is carried out behind you where deer aren't likely to be. On most of the saddles we hunt, our entry/exit routes are split equally between the top of the ridge and the small stream.

Generally speaking, hunting saddles in the hills is not for the faint of heart. Oftentimes you will be hiking up steep, brushy hills, so be sure you are in good condition. Take plenty of clothes with you, too. If a wind comes up a large hollow toward a saddle, it is squeezed down as it approaches the saddle. The saddle serves sort of like a velocity stack in this situation and wind speeds can increase at the saddle and be very brisk and cold. Many times I've rocked and rolled and been chilly in an all-day saddle hunt, only to have my

Because a saddle is up high, a hunter can use the wind effectively when taking stand in a saddle. The author likes to stand in the saddle and use a compass to double check the best wind direction to use for each saddle that he hunts.

lowland hunting friends tell me what a pleasant day it was for them.

Look For The Unlikely

Drive around through a hilly region and you should be able to notice saddles in the hills as you travel along, especially during the winter. These saddles will also be quite obvious on the topo map. Frankly, not all saddles are so easy to recognize. Some are so subtle you may walk right through them and not recognize them for what they are. Others will have such a small drop in elevation they will not be shown on a topographical map.

For instance, in 1996 I was hunting an exceptionally frustrating hilly region. The landscape generally consisted of wide fields or pastures on top of the hilly terrain, and farm fields in the valleys below. The entire area was a series of short ridges jutting out from the high, flat plateaus. Strategic ambush funnels were hard to come by and the topo maps of the territory showed no saddles whatsoever in the region. Still, I had found gigantic rub trees dotting the hardwood hills, tipping me off to the presence of a megabuck.

One day while scouting the finger ridges I noticed a slight dip in the length of one of them. Carefully exam-

Drive around a territory of hills in the winter and saddles in ridgelines can be easily seen through the open timber.

ining the sign there revealed excellent deer movement through this low-key saddle. The trails were scattered about somewhat, making it best for a gun hunt.

I discovered this very slight low spot in late bow season and it was the second Saturday of the firearms season before Carol and I could make a hunt there with a favorable east wind. Slipping into the finger ridge slightly before daylight I put Carol's stand in an ash tree near the saddle. "There's a big buck in this area," I told her, "And if it moves today, this is the place to kill it."

Easing back out of there, I started walking to the north, planning to take a stand on another ridge. By then it was getting light and a shot rang out in front of me. Changing directions, I started to cross a pasture and go to another spot. More shots confronted me and shortly a wild-eyed doe and fawn came bounding across the pasture. Realizing I was practically surrounded by hunters and all my moving was going to do was maybe get a trophy buck killed, I slowly made my way to the edge of the woods and sat down out of harm's way.

As I sat there, shotgun blasts echoed from seemingly every hill and hollow. It was like a war zone. "How could any deer survive here for any length of time," I thought to myself. At about 9:30 a.m. the hills grew eerily silent. Yes, the hunters had gone home, or at least to the restaurants for a late breakfast. To be on the safe side, I stayed put.

At 10:50 a.m. two shots, close together, sounded off from Carol's position. My heart raced; she wouldn't be shooting unless something with good antlers came by. After waiting about 15 minutes I started still-hunting toward her slight saddle. As I came into view of her tree

Carol Herndon killed this 5-1/2-year-old 14-point buck by hunting a small saddle found within the length of a short finger ridge. The deer has an inside spread of 21-1/2 inches.

stand I could see she was still standing up. "Did you get one?" I quizzed her.

"I shot at a good buck," she replied. "I think I hit it. If I did there should be blood just a few feet in front of you."

Walking to where she directed me, I saw a good blood trail. Yes! Following the crimson path slightly over the hill led me right to a beast. "You've killed a monster!" I shouted.

Well, maybe it wasn't a monster, but it was by all means one dandy 5-1/2-year-old buck. The deer's extremely symmetrical 10-point frame carried a 22-1/2-inch inside spread and stayed wide, with the tip-to-tip spread being 18-4/8 inches. It also had nice mass, from

While it's important to teach children about deer sign, make sure you put them in a stand position that deer use often so they don't get bored. Put them in great deer funnels.

A late season snow will plainly reveal where deer trails go and will help you figure out how deer use saddles, points and other terrain features in the hills.

4-1/8 inches to 5-2/8 inches on all circumferences. The rack's only weakness was it was short on height. Every tine had decent length, including the brow tines at 5 inches each, but none were longer than 8-2/8 inches. The deer's gross typical score was 149 inches, net 147 inches even before non-typical deductions of 7-6/8 inches.

These non-typical deductions came from two sticker points on each main beam which were near the base of each brow tine. These points add a beauty and uniqueness to the rack that really sets it off. It also makes it a 14-point buck, something Carol and I have joked about ever since. I don't know about your region of the country, but here in Indiana anyone who sees a huge buck that gets away usually says, "I had a big 14-pointer get away from me!"

"I feel like every time I tell someone I got a big 14-point buck they think I'm telling tales," Carol noted. We still get a chuckle when we talk about this deer, one of many enjoyments we've derived from a hunt which was conducted in a seemingly insignificant dip in a short ridgeline.

Before going on, you might contemplate once more the conditions when this deer was tagged. The region was private land where the landowners let virtually any-

one hunt. Certainly an orange army was assembled that morning and a barrage of shots were fired up until 9:30 a.m. Then the hunters cleared the woods. Just over an hour later, Carol downed the wise, ancient buck. This leads one to believe he was smart enough to know to bed down until the hunters vacated the premises, and then to get up and continue on his search for a hot doe. Was he smart, or just tired? See Cullen Stahl's comments on page 46 before making your final decision.

Over the years, we have set up several other tree stands in saddles that can best be described as subtle. All carry good deer traffic. So while you should be on the lookout for obvious saddles, be sure to check out every subtle feature of the terrain as well. Looking for shed antlers after the season is an enjoyable way to do this. This allows you to take the time to study every aspect of the terrain and how whitetails move about in relation to it.

The saddle where I got a crack at The Hill Buck is actually a high, very narrow saddle on top of a rocky ridge with poor soil. It's not a very "deery" looking place, in other words. Despite this, the contour lines on a topographical map do reveal its presence. I'll admit to you that in 1986 when I was studying the hills near The Home

MY FAVORITE STAND

I love deep woods hunting. Sure it's hard work to trudge a mile or two back in the hills; at times such a hunt will tax every muscle in your body. Once on stand, however, the feeling is hard to beat. Especially if I'm hunting in a saddle, my favorite stand site.

The beauty of the timber gives me a safe feeling, like the trees are going to wrap their branches around me and keep me from harm. Other hunters are rarely found so deep in the woods, so a serene sensation often floods over me. And sitting there knowing my strategic stand position connects thousands of acres on each side of me, all of which could bring forth the buck of a lifetime, makes me tingle with excitement.

Many saddle hunts in the past have produced some of my most memorable hunts. As I age, the day will come when my physical abilities will not allow me to climb the hills, to erect the stand, to extract the deer from its domain. Nevertheless, the memories, the precious memories, will remain: The telltale flick of a tail on the hillside. The flash of sunlight from a tall-tined trophy's antlers as it doggedly follows a doe up the hillside, the terrain pulling both animals to me like metal shavings to a magnet. Yes, shooting from the saddle is something I will always recall.

Brad Herndon

Place, I walked right through the center of this dandy saddle while going to what I thought at the time was a better place to erect my tree stand. Because of the small number of deer in the region, the hardness of the soil, and the absence of rubs and scrapes in the saddle, the deer sign was virtually non-existent to a hunter—me—who was hurriedly walking down the top of the ridge.

Ironically, in early December of the same year, I was sitting in my brown reclining chair at home studying the topo map of the area and I once more noticed the high saddle. While walking through the saddle didn't allow my eyes to believe it was a key deer funnel, logic and looking at the map again did. I knew I had to hunt the high saddle at least two or three times to give it a fair shake. The first hunt I made there in December of 1986 was on a clear, bitterly cold day, at a time of year when the whitetails were yarded up. Amazingly, I saw 11 deer move through the saddle; some came through as late as 11:00 a.m. As the old saying goes, the rest is history.

There have been other times when the map and my mind overrode what I have seen first-hand in the woods. Consider all of your options and leave no stone unturned when trying to figure out the hills. As you will read in other chapters, the hills' undulating, twisting topography contain a fascinating variety of deer funnels. Even so, you will find few of them to be better than a good saddle.

In concluding this chapter, the size of the hilly terrain and the placement of the saddle you are hunting within the hills will determine, to a large degree, what time of day you will see whitetails. My hunting buddies and I have found strategic saddles riding ridgelines deep within the confines of a vast range of hills are great for mid-day hunting. This is true because it takes time for the

deer to filter back to the center of the hills. If the saddles are positioned in smaller sections of hills where farmland is close by, the saddles can produce at any time of the day. Remarkably, though, like so many other locations, the highest percentage of our best trophies taken while shooting from the saddle has been between 10:30 a.m. and 1:00 p.m.

As always, two minds are better than one when it comes to figuring out the best saddles to hunt in hilly areas.

Chapter 6

Hunting
Bench Warmin'
Bucks

The author took this 4-1/2-year-old buck by hunting a bench he found in the hills. The deer's gross typical score is 152 inches.

In moderately hilly areas, benches won't be evident on either aerial or topo maps. This means you will have to walk to discover these key locations. You will find, from time to time, that old lanes will follow these benches. They are excellent places for bucks to make scrapes and rubs.

A bench is an easy terrain configuration to understand since it looks a lot like a park bench. A bench, when it comes to the terminology of terrain, is a relatively flat, level area on a hillside. In hilly regions of moderate height benches may be relatively narrow, perhaps several yards in width. In higher regions such as the Smokey Mountains or the Rockies, these benches can be quite wide, reflective of the size of the terrain in which they are found.

For simplicity's sake, I'll cover benches you might find in moderately hilly land since this is most representative of the type found where whitetails are common.

A bench is used by whitetails because it's the easiest way for them to travel along a hillside. The bench, in hilly terrain, can eventually lead deer up to a saddle or hilltop field funnel. It also can take a deer to the crossover spot on the declining slope of a point. At times it won't take a deer anywhere except along the length of the hill. Each bench is different and should be studied carefully to see what other type of terrain features it con-

nects with, if any. This will determine whether you hunt the bench or not. Sometimes you will hunt the bench. Sometimes the bench will lead you to more advantageous deer travel corridors. Whatever you do, however, don't overlook benches or write them off completely.

In one county adjacent to where we live, there is a series of valleys formed by the glaciers that grindingly pushed through Indiana thousands of years ago. Finger ridges are very evident in this region. Points are numerous, saddles are non-existent, and there are a few hilltop field funnels scattered around. Where long curving hillsides skirt the perimeter of the large flat plateaus found in the county, a few benches are found within their lengths. None of these benches are wide enough for the contour elevation lines on a topographical map to reveal their presence. Likewise, an aerial map is of no use in finding them, either. Walking is the best way to discover them in moderately hilly topography.

In the vast high country of the mountains, it's a different story. Topo maps will reveal where many benches are located simply because their width will be indicated

Powder or even milkweed plant seeds will detect the slightest change in wind movement. This is an excellent way to visually see how wind directions change on the side of hills or in gully bottoms.

by two elevation contour lines being spaced farther apart than others on the hillside. With a little study you will recognize these benches.

When To Hunt A Bench

This isn't an easy decision. As you know by now, a bench will be found quite some distance lower than the land above it. This means the wind can be a menace to your hunting strategies, depending on how the hillside bench is located in relation to the wind direction. Wind speed enters into the formula, too, since it will determine, to a large degree, whether the wind will "curl" in this location. To put it mildly, you best know how the wind flows on hillside benches if you want to taste suc-

cess close to these deer traveling lanes. Obviously the way to learn how the wind works in this type of terrain is to study all you can about the wind, and then go hunting. My strategies in the following hunt may help you in forming a game plan for benches.

As I've already mentioned I always stay high, if at all possible, when hunting trophy whitetails in hilly regions. I've messed up on so many deer I've tried hunting down low in gullies, or on the sides of hills, that it would take a calculator to figure it up. Regardless of this, in the county I mentioned earlier in this chapter that contained few saddles, hilltop field funnels, or other good funnels, I did discover a nice-looking bench. Less than a mile from this bench there was a good funnel to hunt, but Carol was sitting in it, leaving me with trying to use the tricky winds on the bench.

Illustration 6.1 shows a topographical drawing of part of the territory where the bench was positioned. You can get an idea of what I was dealing with. Looking at the bottom of the drawing, you will see a point that drops down and peters out at a small stream. You will notice one deer trail on top of the point coming down and joining three other trails near the base of the point. Where this intersection point is, designated as B in a circle, there was a massive scrape, with a rub tree nearby to match. As you might imagine, my adrenaline level soared when I discovered this hub of deer trails. I considered hunting there, even though it was low where the wind would change from time to time.

Continuing my study of the region, I ventured farther to the north from the hub. I crossed a small stream and noticed three more deer trails coming around the base of another point and joining the main trail I was on. Fifty more yards of walking revealed a slight trail looping over the end of the point a little higher. It too joined my main trail. So now I actually had eight trails funneling into one trail, a trail traveling directly down the bench I previously mentioned. This single trail followed the bench for perhaps 100 yards before trails started fingering off every so often.

I liked what I saw. The fact I found brushy bedding regions both north and south of the key bench trail fired me up even more. I decided to erect my stand at the location shown as an H in a circle on the map. My plans were to sit stand only when the wind was out of the east. Even then I knew the wind might be tricky, so I planned one early hunt to see how much it might switch on me.

Would The Strategy Work?

On November 2 I made my way toward the stand a little after daylight. I had to come in from the east across a field because I couldn't obtain permission to cross the

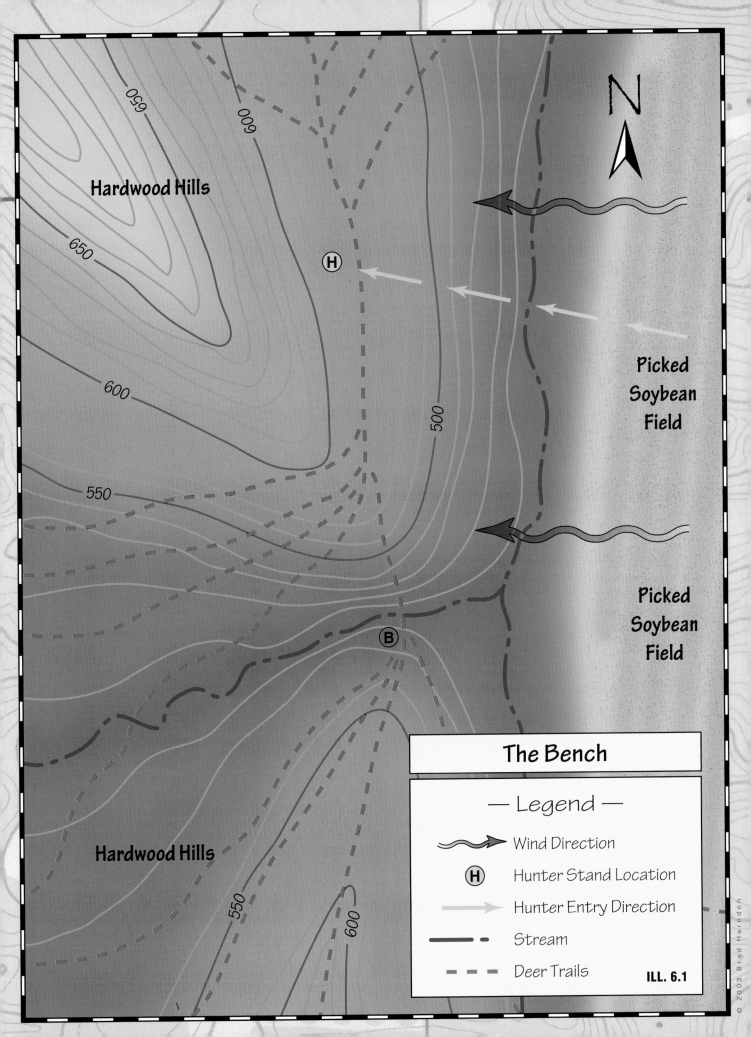

N

Hardwood Hills

650

600

650

600

550

Hardwood Hills

550

600

500

H

B

Picked Soybean Field

Picked Soybean Field

The Bench

— Legend —

Wind Direction

(H) Hunter Stand Location

Hunter Entry Direction

– · – Stream

– – – Deer Trails

ILL. 6.1

property to the west, a better way to approach stand. This meant I had to cross the deer trail, something I try to avoid if at all possible. Nevertheless, the morning hunt proved to be encouraging. I saw a few deer, and better yet, the wind was workable. It changed direction only occasionally, being in my favor about 90 percent of the time. I could live with those odds.

The next predicted light east wind was on November 7. As before, I crossed the picked soybean field right after daylight, giving the whitetails a chance to clear the open area. By 7:00 a.m. I was in my tree and ready. I planned on hunting until at least 1:00 p.m. since the rut would start cranking up before long and I knew the buster bucks would be moving around. I had a lot of con-

Speed ladders are a fast and safe way of putting up your tree stands. On most public lands screw-in steps can't be used, so ladders and rope-on steps must be used.

When traveling along a hillside, whitetails will naturally use benches because they are flat and make for easy walking.

fidence, since I felt a mature buck would use the bench trail I was on if he went from one bedding area to another to check for hot does.

When 9:30 a.m. rolled around I had not yet seen a deer. Although I didn't know it then, later in the day I would talk to hunters who had quit around that time because "...the deer weren't moving". Shortly thereafter, a yearling buck came chasing a doe and two fawns across the field toward the southwest. An hour later the scene was reenacted, only this time a dandy 8-pointer

was doing the harassing. In fact, he made a couple of circles around the field before racing to the base of the point where the large rub and scrape was located. "Aha!" you might be thinking, "I knew he should have hunted the scrape."

Actually, deer can, and do, go anywhere they want to, especially during the rut. I still felt confident in my location, especially as the sun neared its zenith, for I knew it was getting time for the big boys to move. Around 11:45 a.m. I had searched the hardwoods to the south without

When you really get sharp about understanding how the wind flows in a hilly region, you can actually use a wrong wind direction to hunt a bench. Be patient, though, since advancing to this degree takes considerable time for most deer hunters.

seeing anything. Turning my head slowly to the north, white antlers flashed in the sunlight. A buck netting 135 to 140 was closing in on me! My body seemingly became numb as I placed my release on the bowstring.

The buck was moving steadily, stopping every so often to study his surroundings. There was no doubt he was looking for does. Once he gazed directly at me, almost causing my heart to stop. At 12 yards I released an arrow. Every time I see a deer I think I will be more composed when it comes time to shoot, but I'm not. I'm tore up like a train wreck. Regardless of this, I had made a good hit, allowing the deer to travel only 120 yards before expiring.

As the picture in this chapter shows, although not a monster, it's a nice deer. His typical frame grosses 152 inches, netting 144-5/8 before deducting for a split brow tine and another sticker. Final net is 138 inches even.

This is one of my more enjoyable bow kills since I put so much study into how to hunt the buck. One of the keys was using the five trails coming off the point as a funnel leading into the bench trail. The trails from the other point coming into the main bench trail was icing on the cake. Patience in waiting for the ideal wind was important, too, as was staying on stand until midday.

The Master Makes Another Hunt

Jay Mellencamp knows about benches and how whitetails use them — and he's also an expert at using some unlikely wind directions. This knowledge comes from some deep thinking over 42 years of chasing whitetails. He is one of the few hunters I know who can use a bad wind to crank out a productive hunt. One particular hunt he made comes to my mind.

The wind was out of the west, blowing at a steady 20 mph. This is quite brisk, almost enough to curtail deer movement in a section of the country not used to high wind. Mellencamp, as always, laid out his topo map that morning and considered his options for the day. He had a saddle or two he could hunt, a few hillside field funnels, and several points that might produce a keeper buck. Oddly, after considering what was available to him he decided to hunt a bench on the side of a hill that ran more than two miles. This hillside was steep where the bench was located, with either soybean or corn fields at the top and bottom of it. A stream wandered along the bottom edge of the hillside as its companion.

Walking in from the west, Mellencamp crossed a picked soybean field and eased just inside the timber. Although he was actually on top of the hillside, he could see the bench about 60 yards below him, just a good shot distance with his muzzleloading rifle. He placed his stand in a nearby tree and was soon ready for any action the day might bring. Actually he had picked this precise position for a reason. A few days before, a buddy driving through the valley on a nearby road had seen an excellent buck in one of the fields. Mellencamp was hoping this trophy was still in the vicinity. If it was, it should take the deer trail on the bench when it traveled from one section of the hills to another.

The wind stayed brisk and steadily out of the west all morning, just as predicted. Nothing of consequence happened until around 10:30 a.m. The only things moving included a few squirrels burying nuts and the usual amount of tweety birds flitting around. Then Mellencamp's number came up. Walking at a brisk pace, what looked like a 4-1/2-year-old 8-point buck came hurriedly along the bench trail. Mellencamp noticed it had decent height and good mass. Additionally, the deer had a long, unique point, almost a third main beam, growing off the base of its right main beam. It was definitely a shooter, and Mellemcamp put it on the ground.

If you read this article closely, you may have thought Jay Mellencamp was hunting like a novice. Yes, he was hunting with a 20 mph west wind, and, yes, he was hunting with the wind to his back as he watched the deer trail on the bench! Not a smart move, it seems, so why did it work?

Again, understanding the wind and how it works in hilly terrain came into play. The wind, while brisk, always remained steady. Mellencamp told me he had hunted this location before, and with a steady wind of this speed, it actually formed a vacuum over the hill, causing the wind down low on the bench to come back toward him. I'll admit it appears he should have hunted the bench trail from the east side. This way he could have approached from the bottom side by crossing first the field, and then the creek. This way he could have erected his stand on the east side of the trail and used the west wind.

Wisely he didn't, for he knew the wind would have been curling from the east at this point. I use this hunting story because it's a great example of why understanding how the wind flows in regard to hills is so critical to deer hunting success. Sure, gambling like this is a hit-or-miss endeavor at times. Nevertheless, as Mellencamp once told me: "If you learn something from every big buck you mess up on, as time goes on you are going to become one fine deer hunter."

Yes, learning to properly hunt benches is tough. Nonetheless, if you can learn from your mistakes, it's another piece of the hunting puzzle you can put in place.

Chapter 7

Cutting Corners:
Simple Yet
Strategic

Carol Herndon tagged this dandy 8-point buck in an inside corner during the 1999 season. Hunting smart and staying on stand through mid-day were keys to her success.

The morning sun brushed a rich, amber color across the hardwood hills of southern Indiana. It was November 1999 and the fall day was going to be like so many others before it—hot and dry. My wife, Carol watched the forest beneath her tree stand, scanning slowly from side to side, looking for the any telltale sign of deer movement.

Except for some suspicious noise over the hill around 9:30 a.m., the entire morning passed without any movement. Finally the sun reached its zenith and had begun its slow journey west. The temperature by then had soared into the 60s. Most people would say it was way too hot to expect any deer movement at the midday hour. But Carol knew better. She checked her watch. It was 12:55 p.m.

Looking up to once more study the nearby deer trails, Carol saw movement in the closest cedar trees. Tall tines flashed in the sunlight. A shooter buck! And he was closing fast. Raising her 20-gauge shotgun, Carol had trouble getting on the buck because of brush. She focused on an opening barely 15 yards away, and squeezed off the shot as the deer's chest filled the crosshairs. The buck bolted for about 70 yards, then stopped broadside in an opening. A second 20-gauge slug slammed into the deer's chest. He staggered a few feet and went down.

Getting down from her stand, Carol quickly made her way to examine the deer. It had a tight, 8-point rack with good height, good mass, and decent main beam length. It was obvious the deer was mature. He had a massive body, a broad chest, and a large muscular neck. To put it mildly, Carol was one happy hunter.

Consistency Counts

The deer Carol shot turned out to be a 4½-year-old buck. While it wasn't a monster whitetail, it did gross in the 130s and netted 128 inches. After field-dressing it weighed 200 pounds. This was certainly a dandy deer for the area of Indiana we hunt, and most hunters would consider it to be a trophy, one they would be very happy with.

This is important not because Carol killed a big deer, but because it is part of a pattern. From the same stand Carol killed an 11-pointer in 1998, a 9-pointer in 2000, and in 2001 she missed an opportunity on an excellent 8-pointer during bow season. In the four years she's hunted this location, she's had a crack at a mature buck every year. This is the type of consistency we're after.

The terrain feature where Carol had her stand positioned is called an inside corner. This particularly productive inside corner, incidentally, contains very little deer sign. Several people who I've shown this location to say they would never place a tree stand there. But the results speak for themselves.

When hunting an inside corner, be sure to pick your tree stand position carefully so you will be able to use the wind in your favor.

Huge rubs and scrapes are exciting to look at, but most often they aren't located in the best ambush locations within the terrain. You'll harvest more deer by keying in on terrain funnels that choke deer movement down to one specific location.

Location, Location, Location

I love to look at deer sign. Nothing excites me quite as much as looking at a huge scrape; one where dirt is thrown for several feet. Likewise, a huge rub sends my heart rate up, too. Even though I like to find sign, most often I don't end up hunting anywhere near it. The sign just tells me that at least one trophy buck is using the region. Once I know he's in the neighbor-hood, I check my maps for key terrain features that will funnel deer down to a narrow spot. Although location is everything, it takes great confidence to sit on a stand in an inside corner, saddle, or other key choke point where there is seemingly little deer sign. You get that confidence by seeing big bucks come by. Whether you like the looks of a new funnel location or not, don't ever write it off until you've hunted it at least three times under ideal conditions.

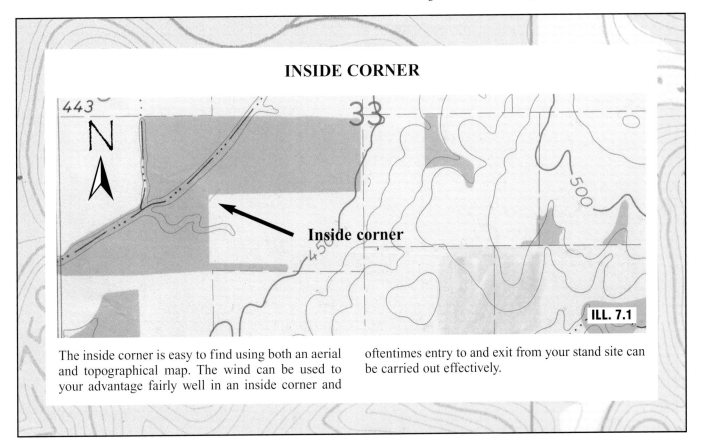

INSIDE CORNER

Inside corner

ILL. 7.1

The inside corner is easy to find using both an aerial and topographical map. The wind can be used to your advantage fairly well in an inside corner and oftentimes entry to and exit from your stand site can be carried out effectively.

Topographical And Aerial Maps

Inside corners are easily recognizable on both topographical and aerial maps. They can be found in flat and hilly terrain of all types and are usually formed by farm fields and pastures. Check out **Illustration 7.1** and you will see a picture of what an inside corner looks like on a topographical map. It will look exactly the same on an aerial map of the same area. There are, however, differences between topographical (topo) maps and aerial maps.

The primary difference between the two maps involves elevations. Aerial maps reveal only general configurations of the terrain, not elevations. In other words, if you find an inside corner on an aerial map, you generally can't tell if the land surrounding this position is hilly or flat. With the topographical map, meanwhile, you can tell exactly what type of terrain you're in.

On the standard 7.5-minute series quadrangle map that most hunters use, these elevation contour lines represent 10-foot changes in elevation. Therefore, if you discover an inside corner on a topo map and it has several contour lines close together, you're looking at a steep hill dropping off near the inside corner. The closer the contour lines are, the steeper the hill. If the contour lines are far apart, they represent a gradually sloping hill.

If you are new to topographical maps, simply take a topo map to an area you generally hunt in and walk

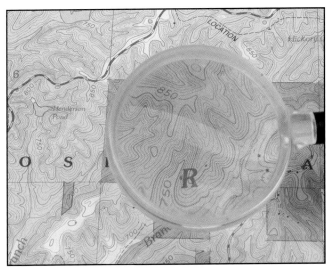

Each elevation contour line on the standard 7.5-minute series topographical maps designates a 10-foot change in elevation.

around with the map in hand. Stop occasionally and study the map versus the place you are standing. With a little work, you will begin to understand what the contour lines on the map represent. You also should begin to visualize what the terrain looks like in an area you are unfamiliar with simply by looking at the topo map. This will prove invaluable when you are checking out a new territory, especially another state you may be planning to hunt.

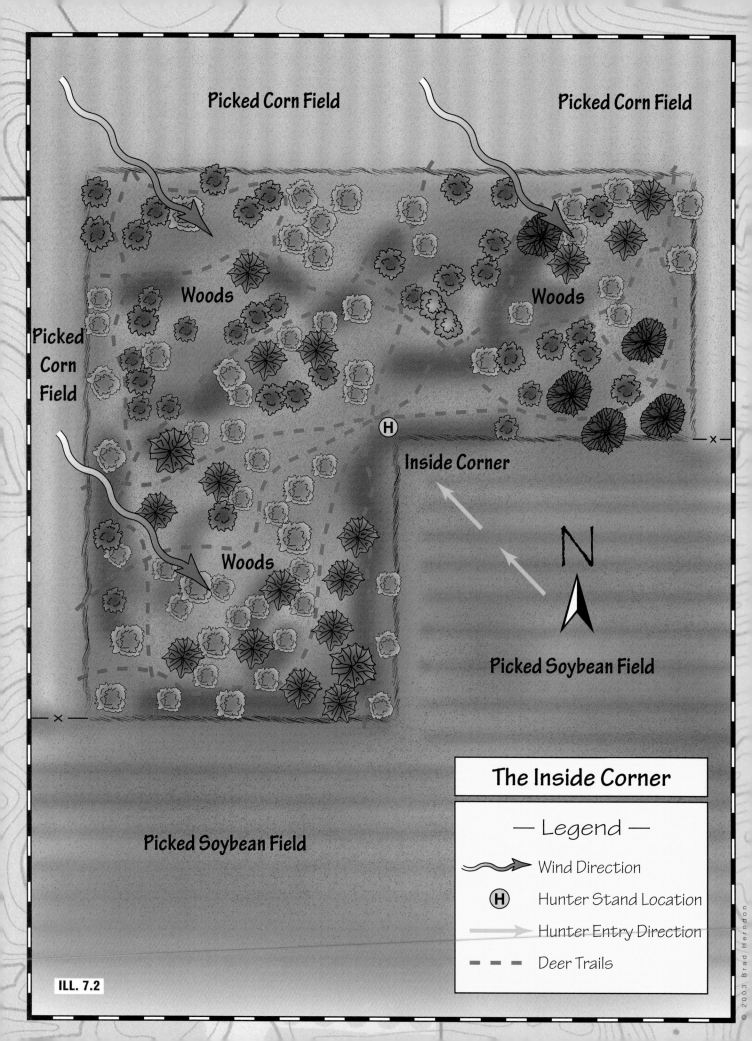

Picked Corn Field

Picked Corn Field

Picked Corn Field

Woods

Woods

Woods

Inside Corner

N

Picked Soybean Field

Picked Soybean Field

The Inside Corner

— Legend —

Wind Direction

(H) Hunter Stand Location

Hunter Entry Direction

- - - Deer Trails

ILL. 7.2

© 2003 Brad Herndon

If an inside corner isn't close to a road, deer will infrequently "pop" the corner instead of staying inside of the woods.

With this discussion out of the way, let's see why an inside corner is a hot stand location, and see by looking at **Illustration 7.2** how deer typically use this terrain feature.

The Inside Corner Is A Hot Spot

Let's assume we have a huge wood formed in the shape of an "L". If we look at this wood from above, we will see it has five outside corners and only one inside corner. The inside corner is hot because whitetails will "cut" around this corner when traveling from one end of the wood to the other during daylight hours. Doing this allows deer to remain unseen from nearby roads because they can stay inside the timber as they move. On the other hand, it affords them the quickest travel route from one end of the wood to the other. This is especially important to a trophy buck when he is out during the tail end of the rut checking for any doe that might still be in heat. The bigger the wood, of course, the more deer traffic you should expect in this location.

Inside corners are what I call half funnels. They channel deer down to a specific, high-odds location, and for the patient hunter knowing how to use the wind wisely,

If you're just starting out using a topographical map, your learning curve will be shorter if you go to a familiar hunting region and study the map as you walk around in terrain you already know.

If you are bow hunting and sense a buck might "pop" the corner before it gets to the inside corner, use a grunt or doe bleat call to bring him within shooting range. This usually isn't a problem for a firearm hunter because he has greater shooting range.

this type of ambush site will be a consistent producer of deer of all types year after year. Some of the best inside corners will be found near roads because traffic of any type will help keep the deer inside the timber when skirting around the corner. This will give you the most ideal shot, especially if you are a bow hunter.

When hunting inside corners in remote, hidden areas, be alert for deer that might occasionally "pop" the corner. In these regions there may not be houses or roads nearby, so deer don't feel as threatened in the open. What I'm saying here is that sometimes deer that are ready to cut the corner in these areas will get so anxious to get to the other side of the corner, they will cut across the corner of the field instead of using the timber in the corner. This puts them behind you if you are hunting directly in the corner near the field.

I have had this happen from time to time, especially in archery season when the whitetails aren't pressured much. A little soft calling with doe bleats or buck grunts oftentimes will still pull them past the stand. I've been successful doing this numerous times. In most states, you won't encounter this small problem of deer "popping" inside corners during gun season. This is true for the simple fact the hunting pressure is high enough that the deer know better than to be caught in an open field.

If possible, put your tree stands up early in the season. This gives you an opportunity to pick the best location and also enables you to choose an entry method that doesn't cross any deer trails.

To assist you in understanding how whitetails typically use inside corners, I have inserted a map, **Illustration 7.2**. This map shows how the deer trails would most often look near an inside corner. It also shows what the perfect approach to the stand is for a hunter, and the ideal stand position, whether it be a ground blind or a tree stand. And don't overlook the wind direction the hunter needs to use. As the map shows, with a northwest wind the hunter could enter from the southeast through the picked soybean field and make a perfect approach to his stand site. If the wind remained steady, he could stay on stand all day and never be detected by any deer passing by. That, folks, is what we're after, the most effective hunt for the strategic terrain feature we are sitting in.

Granted, there are other options we could consider. If the wind was from the southeast the hunter could come in through the field with the wind, cross the deer trail cutting the inside corner and take his stand on the northwest, and downwind side, of the best corner trail. Yes, this leaves the hunter downwind of the inside corner

By hunting strategic places and using the wind properly, you can more easily capture your son or daughter's first bow kill on film.

What To Do With The Wind

Don't forget a critical fundamental element of whitetail hunting: You must stay downwind of deer to be consistently successful. For those of you who are just beginning in your pursuit of the whitetail, you now have available to you a wealth of information about deer, both biological and tactical. Through magazines, books, videos and the Internet, you can read and watch to your heart's content.

Your learning curve will be rapid using these resources, although you may inadvertently be led astray to a degree if you're not careful. For example, you will read about cover scents designed to keep deer from smelling you. Likewise, clothes and boots that block human scent from escaping into the atmosphere will catch your eye as well. With all of these products, it sounds like it will be a simple matter to kill a deer. Just buy these products, put them on, spray a little cover scent from head to toe, then go out and drop a big, old buck.

Sorry, it isn't so simple. While these products do work well, they aren't foolproof. This is true because you are dealing with an animal with an extraordinary nose. This is why we can't make mistakes when hunting. Implementing sound hunting methods and wise use of the wind still are the key ingredients in tagging whitetails every year.

Deer attractants aren't a magic formula for success, either. Every year I have at least one small buck that has crossed my entry trail track me to stand. Bucks don't do this because I'm using a deer attractant, since I don't use these products. The young, naive deer is trailing me down because he has come across a different smell and is curious as to what it is and where it's going. Fawns will often do this, as well, especially button bucks.

In a similar vein, I remember a hunt I made on a very hot morning a few years back. I wore only a short-sleeved shirt while walking in to the stand and was profusely sweating by the time I reached my hunting site. Later that morning I watched a 2½-year-old buck come in and lick a small sapling near me. He was really enjoying himself, but it wasn't because I had any fabulous deer lure on. He was, quite interestingly, savoring the salt my sweaty arms had deposited on the sapling.

What I'm saying with all this is, first and foremost, learn how to hunt in strategic locations, using the wind to your advantage the best you can. I have nothing against any of the products mentioned, nor am I questioning the fact they are effective. They will reduce your odds of getting winded; they just don't work to perfection yet. By all means you can wear and use these products if you desire, ***but you should hunt as if they had never been invented.*** Now let's delve into another tricky subject regarding the wind.

trail. But it also means his scent is spewing behind him out into the woods for hundreds of feet. There could be deer there — possibly a nice buck — that could detect his scent and ruin the hunt.

And then consider the hunter has walked directly across the hot deer trail in the corner. What if a doe comes traipsing along and detects where he has crossed the trail? Most often she will turn around and go back in the direction from which she came. And what happens if a monster buck is a few minutes behind her, following her track? Simply put, he'll follow her trail where she avoided the corner and the hunter won't even see him. Certainly the options I've just discussed are not perfect hunts. About this time, I have a suspicion that a few of you might be thinking. "I'll just put on my clothes that prevent my scent from escaping into the atmosphere, apply some of my favorite cover scent for good measure and hunt the inside corner the way I want to." Let me address this issue.

This dad is doing a smart thing. He's placing his son's stand site on high ground where the wind can be wisely used to the hunter's advantage.

Strategic Stand Sites And Hilly Land

A strategic terrain funnel — even an inside corner that carries heavy deer traffic — isn't always a hot stand location. Here's why.

Let's suppose you have obtained permission to hunt in a new tract of timber in a hilly region. Taking out your topographical map of the area, you discover a nice looking inside corner near some farm fields in the bottom of a valley. After driving to the area, you walk directly to the inside corner and are elated by what you see. There are three deer trails skirting the inside corner, all close together and heavily used, and huge deer tracks dot each trail. In your excitement, you may think to yourself, "This is an incredible place to hunt!"

It isn't. Unless you understand exactly how wind flows in hilly regions. And even then you must be tremendously patient regarding how and when you can hunt such a location. When you first start deer hunting in hilly regions, you should always stay up high on plateaus, ridgetops, and these sorts of places. The wind on top of the hilly regions blows consistently from the predicted direction for the day. Down low in hollows and gullies, the wind switches

If you desire to, you can use scent-eliminator products. Don't, however, rely on these products to replace sound hunting strategies.

Every year, inside corners produce Pope & Young bucks for many bow hunters throughout North America.

directions quite often, and will even swirl. This occurs because of how the wind "washes" over the hilly terrain, and it also is caused by the change in velocity of the wind. Of course these often-changing wind directions allow whitetails traveling through your ambush location to catch your scent quite often, possibly ruining a hunt.

This can only be experienced by hunting down low and seeing how often the wind switches. It can be maddening, especially if you know a good buck is using the area. Even as many years as I've hunted, most of my hunts in hilly regions take place on high ground.

Regarding hilly regions and wind directions, the height of the hills will determine how the wind flows. The wind may switch slightly differently when it comes over a 50-foot high hill than it does over a hill 200, 500, or 1000 feet in height. Keep this is in mind when you hunt hilly regions. Experimentation and careful note-taking is always the rule when learning about any territory containing hills of any size. Most of my hill examples will be similar in height to hilly regions found in portions of Illinois, Indiana, Ohio, Wisconsin, Iowa, Missouri, Minnesota, and regions of many other states.

Switch-hitting Tactics

There is one neat little trick Carol pulled during her hunt at the beginning of this chapter that you should be aware of.

On that particular day I was hunting about a mile away from Carol. When she shot, I said to myself, "She had to

MY FAVORITE STAND

I guess a person's favorite stand will be where that person killed the most big deer. I know it is with me. In my book, nothing beats an inside corner. They're good to hunt in both hilly and flat land. I like an inside corner tucked into a hilly region best, for the simple reason the lay of the land is so beautiful. I enjoy being in the corner and glancing off in the distance and seeing a stately buck trotting across an open field, seemingly oblivious to what's going on around him. Even though I won't get a shot, just knowing he's there gives me an optimistic feeling.

I like the way I can get into a stand in an inside corner. Most of the time I wait until it's starting to get a little light before I start in. This means the deer have cleared the field I'll be crossing and I can slip right in there undetected. An inside corner makes it pretty easy to use the wind in, too. That's vitally important. Every corner I hunt doesn't have great deer sign. Some do, some don't.

Sign doesn't mean too much to me, though, because I know if a big deer is in the area, there's a very good chance he might come by my stand at any time of the day.

I always hunt until 1:00 p.m. when the rut is going good. I've tagged good bucks at inside corners during all periods of the day, from early morning until late evening. I've taken most of my trophy whitetails from inside corners during the midday period. I didn't like it when I was a little girl, but nowadays I don't mind standing in a corner at all.

Carol Herndon

INSIDE CORNER

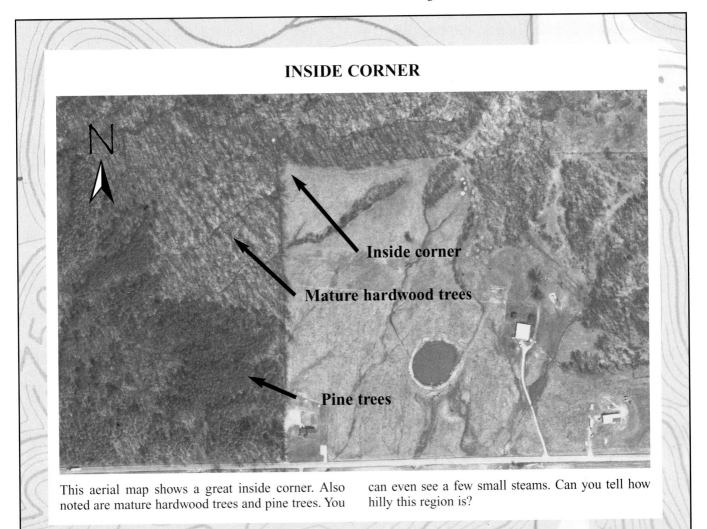

This aerial map shows a great inside corner. Also noted are mature hardwood trees and pine trees. You can even see a few small steams. Can you tell how hilly this region is?

change tree stands. There's no way she was going to kill a deer at this time from the place she started out in this morning." I suspected this because the wind was predicted to change from northwest to easterly during the morning. Before leaving the house that morning, I had checked what type of pressure system we were dealing with and had taken an educated guess as to how the wind would change.

Later on in the day when I met Carol at her hunting location I quizzed her. "Did you get a deer?"

"Yes, I did, a nice one." she replied. "Did you change stands about 10:30 a.m.?" I said.

"I sure did," she replied. "The wind switched fairly quickly between 10:00 a.m. and 10:30 a.m., as predicted, and with the east wind I knew I wasn't going to see any deer from where I was sitting. I unloaded my gun, took my equipment over to the stand on the west side of the inside corner and everything worked to perfection. The deer never had a clue I was around. If I had stayed on the other side, I believe he would have winded me and slipped back over the hill without me ever knowing he was around."

What she did was a brilliant move, at exactly the correct time. And I told her so.

Maybe at this point you're starting to pick me apart a little. If you are, it's exactly what I want you to do. This means you're thinking. Yes, Carol did have to cross the deer trail in order to get to the other tree stand, and this was somewhat of a gamble. Still, it was much better than staying in her initial tree stand position. Fortunately the first deer through was a trophy whitetail.

Perhaps you're also thinking about how I said a hunter's scent would be scattered back in the woods if she hunted on the other side of the trail going through the inside corner. This is true, especially in a flat wood. However, Carol's inside corner was located at the edge of a pasture field on top of a flat hilltop. Just west of the stand she was in, the hill dropped off steeply. Few deer use the bottom of this hill and the light east wind sailed her scent gently off into never-never land to the west. So while Carol's hunt wasn't what would be considered the perfect hunt, she had executed the hunt as well as anyone could, and it resulted in her tagging a beautiful 8-point buck.

Learn the rules, then make them work for you.

Chapter 8

Double Inside Corners

Different, But

Dynamite

The Double Inside Corner is an area where two inside corners are in close proximity. You'll find these from time to time on a topographical or aerial map and the strategies required to successfully hunt these areas differ a bit from the simple inside corner. **Illustrations 8.1** and **8.2** show what double inside corners look like on a topographical map and reveals the difference between inside corners and double inside corners. Although the double inside corner appears to function in the same manner as it's single cousin, the double corner leaves the hunter with questions, and some tough choices.

First of all, which of the double inside corners should he hunt? It appears both can be good stand placement locations. Secondly, will the hunter be able to use the wind to his advantage when hunting only one of the double inside corners? In answer to this second question, no he won't. Here's why.

In the single inside corner shown in **Illustration 7.2** in Chapter 7, it's easy to see how ideal a northwest wind is for the hunter. Conversely, hunting the same type of corner in **Illustration 8.1** presents a problem. Sure the hunter's scent is blown out into the open field behind him with a northwest wind. This seems great. However, since the double inside corners are close together, his scent will be carried diagonally across the short width of the field and into the woods on the other side. Some of the deer using the opposite inside corner would smell him as they traveled north and south to and from this corner. Hunt the other inside corner with a northeast wind and the hunter encounters the same problem.

Monsters In The Middle

Because of what I've just described, a hunter must wait for nearly perfect wind when hunting double inside corners to pull off the perfect hunt. This takes a lot of discipline. Generally speaking, I've found the point about half way between the double inside corners to be the best position for a tree stand. Once my stand is there, I wait for a wind that will carry my scent directly down the length of the field behind me, parallel with the field edges. This lowers the risk of a whitetail smelling me. As you might imagine, waiting for the wind to come from only one precise direction can be difficult. But wait you must.

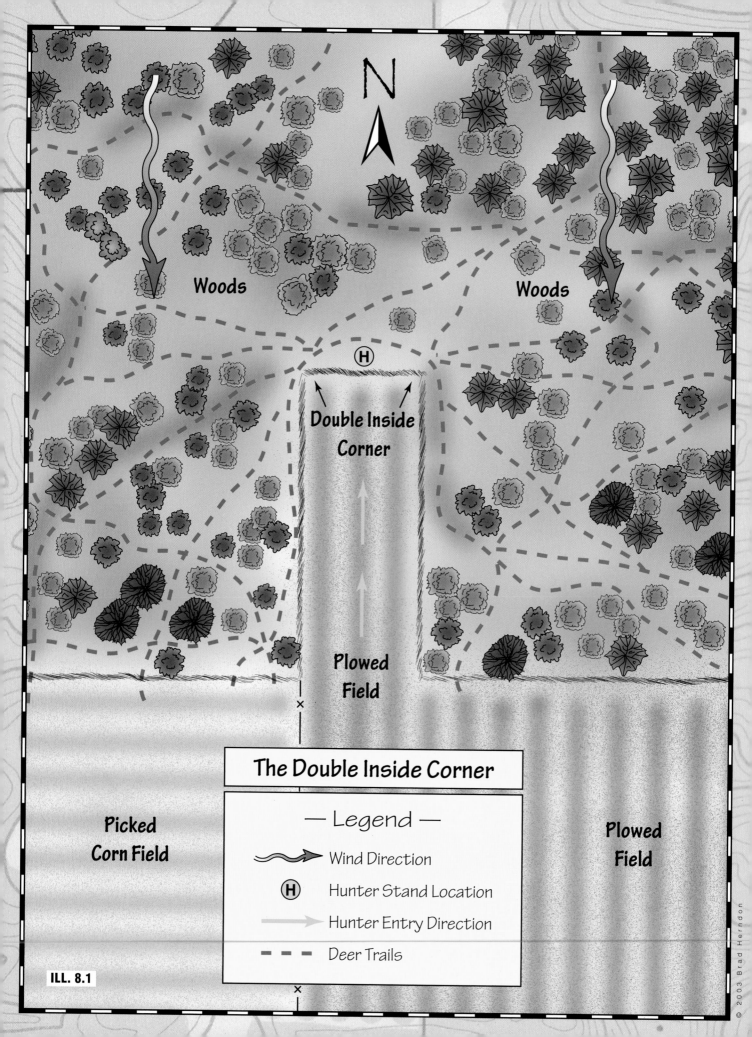

Woods

Woods

Ⓗ

Double Inside
Corner

Plowed
Field

Picked
Corn Field

Plowed
Field

The Double Inside Corner

— Legend —

Wind Direction

Ⓗ Hunter Stand Location

Hunter Entry Direction

- - - Deer Trails

ILL. 8.1

© 2003 Brad Herndon

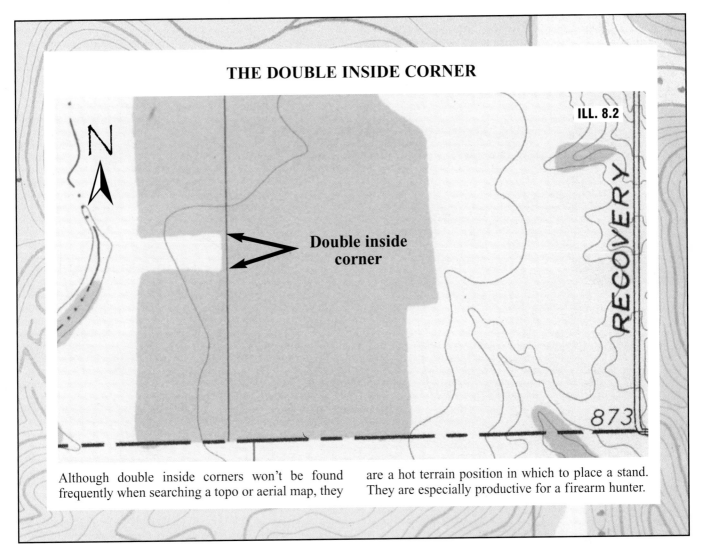

THE DOUBLE INSIDE CORNER

ILL. 8.2

N

Double inside corner

RECOVERY

873

Although double inside corners won't be found frequently when searching a topo or aerial map, they are a hot terrain position in which to place a stand. They are especially productive for a firearm hunter.

Waiting for conditions to be precisely right in a deer terrain funnel is why I encourage you to locate a variety of strategic deer travel corridors in the areas you hunt. Line up several stand sites and name each one of them. Carol's Inside Corner, Goldsby Hill, The Y Stand, and The Ledge are a few of the names of our stand sites. Once this is done, note the wind direction, or directions, which can be effectively used with each stand. If you work hard and accumulate several key funnel locations, this will allow you to use the wind to your advantage in at least one of the stand sites on any given day, regardless of what wind direction nature may throw at you. This gives you many options, and guarantees you can always hunt smart.

Going back to our double inside corner map, I should mention it is an exact replication of a hunt I made during the 1983 firearms season in southern Indiana. During the early portion of the rut I had discovered this double inside corner in a region where the land had a gentle roll to it. The terrain didn't look hilly enough to give me major problems with switching wind directions and during firearms season that year I caught a direct north wind one day that enabled me to try this possible new hotspot.

Walking in from the south, I eased up the middle of the field toward a point midway between the inside corners. I slowly eased into the woods about 15 yards. Since I had never before hunted this portion of the county, I was curious as to what kind of deer sign might be there. Even though whitetails were scarce in many portions of Indiana in 1983, I could see a few good rub trees and even a cluster of torn up scrapes. I ascended a tree on the spot.

It was about 2:30 in the afternoon when I was settled comfortably in my tree. At 3:30 p.m. I noticed deer movement to the north. Barging right in, a big buck worked over a scrape, tossing fresh dirt several feet behind him. After leaving scent on an overhanging limb, he walked right past me at barely 15 yards. A well-placed slug from my 12-gauge shotgun dropped him on the spot. He turned out to be a 3½- year-old, 9-point buck weighing a healthy 186 pounds field-dressed.

Since you have greater shooting range with a firearm, spending time in a double inside corner when the wind is favorable will result in lots of filled whitetail tags.

Use a compact range finder to determine your shooting distances at each stand site you have. This takes most of the guesswork out of bow shots.

Not all deer hunts, as we know, are short and sweet like this one. Still, hunting smart pays off. If you hunt double inside corners in a similar manner as I described you will find the location to be productive, especially during firearm seasons. Not only can you cover the area directly in front of you, unless it is extremely brushy, you should oftentimes be able to cover both inside corners if they are fairly close to you. And if you are located on the edge of the wood, you should be able to pick off any whitetail trying to pop either corner and come through the field. For the archer, of course, it's more difficult.

Bow Hunting Double Inside Corners

Even though double inside corners close together aren't encountered as often as single inside corners are, as you study topographical and aerial maps, you will find them from time to time. In 1987 I noticed a couple of inside corners close together in the region where I grew up. I walked through the forest there and found the deer sign to be dismal since the whitetails were just starting to expand into the area. However, since virtually no one hunted the section I decided to let Carol be my scout and test out what kind of whitetail action was going on there during archery season.

She set up between the corners and from the beginning, her hunts were fantastic! Because of the low number of deer, the lack of hunting pressure had allowed the

Hunting terrain traps will give you a crack at the best deer in your hunting territory. Do your part after the shot to recover every deer. When trailing a deer, it's always best to have two experienced people on the trail.

buck/doe ratio to be near 50/50. This forced the antlered deer in the region to be out constantly searching for hot does. Each day she hunted Carol had several sightings of bucks of various sizes dashing about in a rutting frenzy.

Because her stand was halfway between the corners, many of the bucks were out of bow range. Finally, though, one meandered by at 11:30 one morning and she laid it to rest. She still looks back on that bow season as one of her most enjoyable ever, even though the deer she killed was a yearling 7-point.

Upping The Odds In Bow Season

As just related, hunting midway between corners can often result in the archer seeing deer out of his effective shooting range. Even in ideal setups, this still may happen. For instance, there may be three trails skirting around a single inside corner. One may be 20 yards away from the best stand position, while another trail may be 32 yards away, and yet another one 40 yards away.

For the firearms hunter, this isn't any big deal. For the bow hunter, it's a major problem. The two trails farthest away are beyond most bow hunter's effective killing range. Especially if brush is present. Here's a little-used trick to keep this from happening.

In the county south of us there is a saddle that carries nice deer traffic and is ideal for an archery season stand site. With this particular saddle, we have a perfect entry from the north, allowing us to enter the stand without disturbing many deer and to use any wind direction from the south. While checking this saddle two weeks before the 2001 deer season, Carol and I discovered a tree on the south side of the saddle had fallen and blocked the deer trail going through the center of the saddle. Because of this, the whitetails had started going around the south side of the brushy saddle. This prevented any kind of bow shot from being taken from our stand site, and because of the brush a gun shot would have been extremely difficult.

After looking the situation over, we cut some small cedar trees and used them to block the new trail the deer had formed. We placed these blockades roughly

Even though it's a little tougher for an archer because of his limited shooting range, double inside corners are still great locations to ambush mature bucks.

You can improve some deer funnels by altering the trail locations. Cedars and pine trees work well for blocking the old trails.

Late summer is a great time to get out your spotting scope and see if big bucks are living in the region you plan on hunting.

150 yards apart down the length of the saddle. Next we started at these two locations and used our feet to snake a new trail to the saddle, running the trail through the saddle near the top of the fallen tree. This placed the new trail 15 yards from our tree stand, a perfect bow shot.

Carol and I worked our way back and forth on this new trail several times, pushing aside leaves and sticks until the trail was very visible to the eye. I also used my ratchet cutters to trim any limbs projecting out into the new trail. This assured this new trail would be the easiest location for a deer to walk through. Like humans, whitetails will take the path of least resistance.

Less than three weeks later Carol hunted this stand for the first time. She had three bucks come through on the new deer trail that morning, two 1½-year-old bucks and one 2½-year old 8-point buck! Keep in mind all three deer were broadside at 15 yards, and because Carol was using the wind wisely all three bucks were unaware any hunter was near. Because Carol was trying for a bigger buck that fall she passed on these deer. Throughout the year this new deer trail worked to perfection, carrying excellent deer traffic. By building our own terrain funnel, we had turned a disastrous situation into a can't-miss hunting spot.

If the situation warrants it, you can use this trick to change deer trails found within double inside corners, altering them so the trails come closer to the most favorable position for a bow stand. We've altered trails many times throughout the years, in a variety of situations, and it really works. You can use a rake, instead of your feet, to make the new deer trail if you so desire. Both methods will work. As far as blocking the trail, cedars, pines and other evergreen trees will work best since they pile up faster, but any kind of brush piled high enough will do the job.

Double inside corners can be tricky to hunt, but they can also prove to be very productive locations. Seek them out. Scout them effectively and be flexible enough to make the changes that will bring deer within range and you will be successful. When you see a double inside corner, mark that location on your map and make sure you give it a good long look.

Chapter 9
Keying In
On
Points

It's very difficult to comprehend how deer use points in the hills to escape hunters. Two hunters studying maps will usually figure out difficult hunting terrain faster than a single hunter will.

A point in its most basic shape is formed when an isolated ridge runs for some distance—let's say a mile—then slopes gradually down to lower land below. To visualize this, picture a wooden pencil sharpened on one end lying on a table. The pencil is the ridge, the top of it is the ridgetop, its sides are hillsides along the ridge, and the pencil's sharpened point is similar to a point of terrain since it drops down to lower elevations.

Points are little noticed by many deer hunters though they may be abundant in some hilly areas where saddles aren't present and hilltop field funnels are few and far between. We hunt one county containing terrain exactly like this, so we learned how to hunt points, which was an interesting experience. In other cases, points may be found in close proximity to saddles, hilltop field funnels, converging hubs, and other types of topography found in hilly regions. Points will be found in higher elevations, such as mountainous regions, in hills moderate in height, and even in low land areas where they are not so prominent.

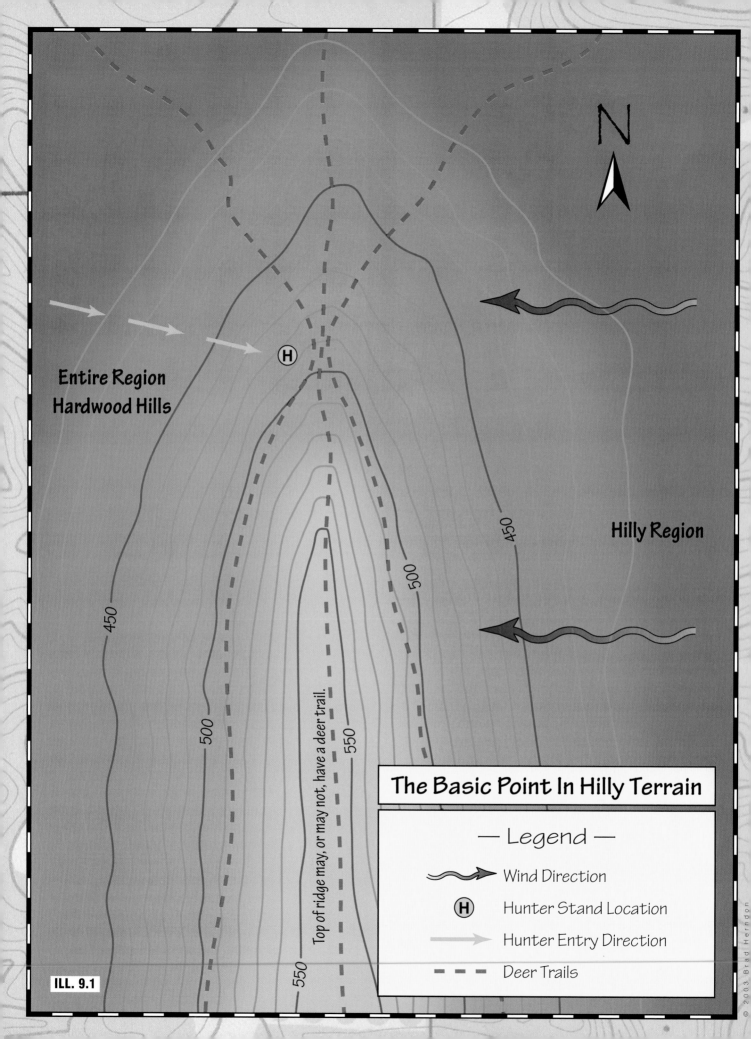

Entire Region
Hardwood Hills

Hilly Region

450

450

500

500

500

550

550

550

Top of ridge may, or may not, have a deer trail.

The Basic Point In Hilly Terrain

— Legend —

Wind Direction

(H) Hunter Stand Location

Hunter Entry Direction

— — — Deer Trails

ILL. 9.1

© 2003 Brad Herndon

Deer have many ways of escaping hunters in the hills, especially by using points.

Illustration 9.1 shows the basic configuration of a point in moderately hilly terrain. Notice the height of the ridge forming the point. It's about 150 feet high, about the height of many points found in southern Indiana and several other midwestern states. I have shown a trail along the side of the hill on each side of the ridge, as well as a deer trail on top of the ridge. The deer trail I've shown on top of the ridge may not exist on many points you run across; it depends on the width, height and general habitat found in the forested tract it lies within.

Notice how as the deer trails along the side of the hill go toward the point that they will eventually cross, since the point is dropping in elevation. The top of the ridge

trail also crosses the two side-hill trails at this junction, so we now have three trails crossing in one spot. This significantly increases your odds of seeing deer. Just as importantly, where the three deer trails cross is on top of the sloping point, a place where the wind can be wisely used to carry your scent away from the deer. The drawing shows the hunter's location, his entry to his stand site, and the wind direction he used.

This drawing shows in simple form how whitetails most often use points of moderate height. This point is relatively easy to recognize and to hunt. As in other types of terrain funnels, your success rate will be largely determined by how careful you are in using the wind. I've

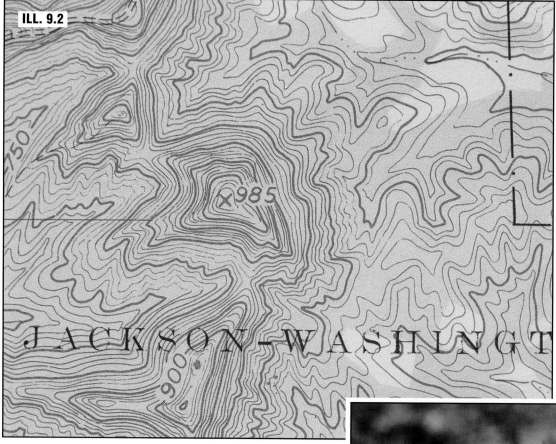

ILL. 9.2

Shown is a topographical map of a moderately hilly region. Can you pick out the saddles within the terrain? How about the points?

Walking your hunting area during late winter and early spring can bring tremendous enjoyment.

found many points to be consistently productive at all times of the year, including early and late seasons. Overall, the rut is the best time to take bucks 3 ½ years of age, and up on a point. On points where the trail at the top of the ridge isn't present, you can, at times, hunt above or below the location where the trails from the side of the hill cross. You must be very mindful of how the trails run in relation to the wind. You have a small margin of error in this setup.

Assuming you now understand the fundamentals of how to hunt the basic point, let's put this point you're hunting, and several others just like it, into a hilly region containing several saddles and see how you react to them.

Learning Where To Hunt

Illustration 9.2 is a picture of a topographical map in a hilly area of public land. With study you should be able to recognize several dandy looking saddles nestled within the ridges. Note that some of them are deep saddles. Saddles, as I pointed out earlier, are the hottest locations in the hills. Quite naturally, then, if you are knowledgeable about hunting hilly terrain, these saddles are where you will spend your time if you are hunting these hills for the first time.

The region shown in **Illustration 9.2** lies directly

behind my house. When I first started hunting these hills in 1985 they contained little deer sign. Nevertheless, it was the home of a deer Carol called The Pine Cone Buck (she saw him while she was picking up pine cones), and we dearly wanted to put him on the wall of our little log home. Unfortunately, I knew little about hunting the hills back then, and most of my time was spent learning the ins and outs of hill hunting. At first I tried hunting rub areas, scrape clusters, and the best looking deer trails, all without much success. Finally I did discover a breakline in the timber and was able to kill two mature bucks with my bow on the breakline trail, including one of the son's of The Pine Cone buck.

Back then I kept looking at the saddles, but the deer sign just didn't look good there. Up high there were few rubs, and no scrapes to get me excited. The timber wasn't even very pretty. It consisted of mostly chestnut (scrub) oak, greenbriers, and barren looking, rocky hills. Despite this lack of enthusiasm for these saddles, reason finally won out and I convinced myself location, not sign, was the most important factor when it came to killing deer. I started hunting the saddles. And they were good to me. But not always. There were years when I knew a real monster buck was using the hills, yet I could never see him. I reasoned deer-hunting pressure was increasing on the public land and this could be a factor.

Still, my approaches to my stand sites in the saddles were solid. Usually I could walk in on a ridge top which contained no deer trail running its length, then simply "drop" into my saddle. This walk did involve going up and down extremely steep hills and was physically taxing. One day when I was coming out from one of my saddle hunts, I learned a lesson on top of one of these steep hills that I want to share with you.

A Hilltop Experience

It was almost 2:00 p.m. as I trudged out along the ridgetop. I carried on my back my tree stand and all of the gear I had used on my morning hunt. My bow was in my left hand. As I reached the bottom of a steep hill, I looked towards its top and decided to charge the hill, just to keep in shape. Head down, legs churning, I moved up the steep incline at a brisk pace. It took concentration, but I made it to the top of the hill without stopping. I felt good about my accomplishment. As I stood resting by the foundation of a 50-year-old wooden fire tower, I noticed a younger guy already standing nearby. He evidently had climbed the hill from another direction on one of the forestry's walking trails.

I was breathing a little hard, but this guy was sweating profusely and his breathing was very labored. I subconsciously thought what a shame it was that a guy several years younger than me was in such terrible shape. We talked for awhile and had a great conversation about the beauty of the area. He noted how enjoyable it was for him to look over the beautiful farm country below from the overlooks the hills contained, especially from The Pinnacle, the highest peak in the region.

When we had both caught our breath, he asked me which way I was going. "I'm going down the hill to the west, to the parking lot," I replied.

If you're going to hunt hilly or mountainous regions, you should be in good condition. Therefore, you should have a consistent walking or running program established during the summer months.

"I'm parked down there, too," he said. "Mind if I walk down with you?"

"Not at all," I remarked, "I'd be glad to share the walk."

We hadn't walked very far until a feeling of humbleness I have rarely experienced overwhelmed me. Tears welled up in my eyes. It was very obvious to me the younger guy had a prosthesis, an artificial leg!

I could only imagine how difficult it was for him to climb hills, to laboriously struggle up the steep inclines in order to get to the hilltops, the only places where the beautiful landscapes could be fully seen, and fully appreciated. Determination, dedication, perseverance; he had it all. He was one special young man who had my complete admiration.

I insert this touching experience because we can, as many of you know, get discouraged when deer hunting. We may be trying to get our first deer without success

If you are going to hunt public land and carry your tree stand in and out, be sure to use one of the lightweight portable stands now on the market.

and get disgusted. "Why can't I get a deer?" It may be our first buck we're trying to tag. "I can kill does, why can't I ever see a buck?" Or our interests may be focused on taking a trophy whitetail and the realization that this is one tough game has sunk in to our thoughts. Hunt after hunt is made, and failure after failure is our bitter reward. At this stage of the game our attitude may be one of only defeat and despair. I know, because even though I'm a very optimistic fellow, in the past my attitude has been lower than a snake's belly during some deer seasons. That's not true anymore.

A positive, confident, attitude is necessary for success. The young guy with an artificial leg had an incredibly optimistic outlook about life. We should, too. And learning how to hunt properly will be an important building block on your way to becoming a confident deer hunter while on stand.

Points: The Whitetail's Great Escape Feature

As I continued to hunt the saddles from time to time in the region behind my home, I tried to be more observant of every detail in the woods. On my walks in and out on the ridgetops, I looked for any deer trails crossing the ridgetop which were not located near the saddles themselves. In a few places I noticed deer tracks up high, well above the saddles, indicating a few whitetails were crossing there. Faint trails were barely evident.

At this point I considered the idea that maybe, just maybe, the biggest bucks in the region had figured me out, instead of me figuring them out. Mature bucks, especially those 5 1/2 years of age and older, become simply brilliant in their movement patterns when they sense the presence of hunters. Sure, I had been careful hunting my saddles. Maybe careful wasn't good enough. I had, after all, left my scent on the ground many times. During their nightly forays, they had to have smelled where I had walked. Maybe they had even picked me off as I sat in the saddles without me ever knowing it.

Thereafter, on each hunt in the saddles, I made a special effort to look up high on the hills in front of me, and even behind me. Two different times one bow season I could see antlers flashing in the hardwoods behind me, up high near the very top of the hill. Both appeared to be mature bucks. Where I sighted these two deer was actually the formation of a point that jutted out

There's nothing more exciting than to find a huge shed antler. You then know the buck you will be after next year is alive and well. And you have plenty of time to figure him out.

to the west. Farther north, on the other side of the ridge where the point started, there was also a faint deer trail. I was beginning to believe deer were using these trails to avoid me when I hunted in the different saddles.

As best as I could tell, the two trails I discovered ran along each side of the point, and then crossed as the point sloped down to the west. I reasoned that taking a stand in this point position during the rut should bring out the truth, or folly, of my theory.

Thus, one morning in gun season I made a blind entry into this location. I knew the area well enough, I thought, to go up a small stream, then ease up the side of the point to the north, where I would erect my stand. The north wind I had would carry my scent back away from the point crossing, allowing me to hunt as though invisible. When daylight came I realized I had made a mistake. I could tell by

A still-hunter who knows how whitetails use terrain to move from funnel to funnel can kill some big bucks. This hunter, Junior Stuckwisch, has taken a number of great bucks by still-hunting hilly regions.

the shape of the hillside on my side of the point that I was too far away from where the deer trail would cross over the slope of the point. I needed to be 100 yards closer.

I begrudgingly sat there for some time before getting the ambition to take my stand down and move up the hill. Working quietly, I removed the stand and let it down to the ground. I removed the rope-on steps and placed them in my pack. Placing the stand and the pack on my back, I started inching up the hill, watching as I walked. Within a few steps, movement to the east caught my eye. Blasting down the hillside trail along the point, a small buck ripped past me, crossed the slope of the point and was gone. Seconds later a doe made the same trip. "Hmmm," I thought. "A doe chasing a buck. Something's going on here." I readied my shotgun.

I saw him coming! The buck had a huge rack with tall tines. If he followed the same path as the other deer did, I would have an excellent shot at him. However, being experienced, he knew the other deer had popped over the point, so rather than go that way, he took a shortcut directly up the hill in order to cut the doe off. He was going fast

and the shot was over 100 yards, beyond my shooting abilities. I watched as he disappeared out of sight.

This hunt is a classic example of how trophy whitetails can use points to avoid hunters in hilly terrain. Even though I wasn't successful, I had come extremely close to knocking down a real brute, and I had added one more piece of knowledge to my bag of tricks. **Illustration 9.3** shows how the deer were avoiding me in the saddle, and how they were using the point where I had the close encounter. I have drawn this map in a very simple fashion so it roughly resembles the topo map picture in **Illustration 9.2**, the area where I was hunting. This same map shows another hunt I'll cover in the next few paragraphs, too.

Concerning the point hunt I just discussed, notice the deer trails along the point and how high they are above the two saddles shown. This enabled the whitetails to avoid me and generally stay out of my sight. The tree stand site designated by a P is where I was located, a little too far away from the crossing location on the point, which was why I had to move.

Unfortunately, I was injured shortly after this hunt and missed the rest of that deer season. In addition, the next year no evidence showed up to indicate this deer was still alive, so for a few years I concentrated most of my hunting efforts in other territories harboring better bucks.

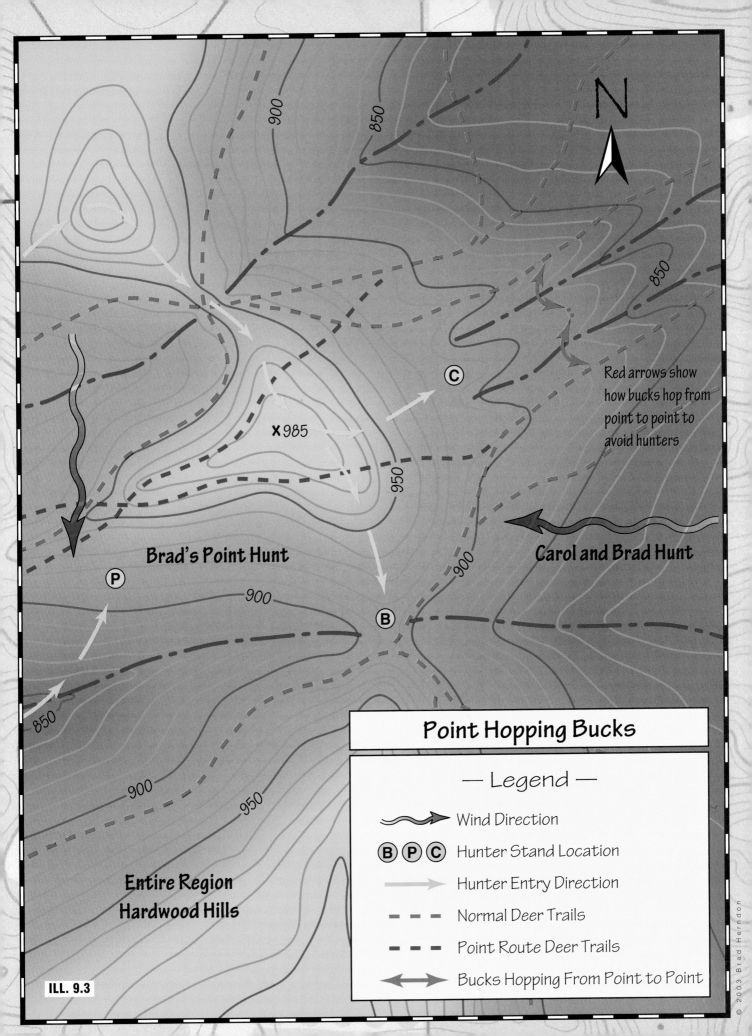

Red arrows show
how bucks hop from
point to point to
avoid hunters

C

X 985

Brad's Point Hunt

Carol and Brad Hunt

P

900

850

950

900

Entire Region
Hardwood Hills

ILL. 9.3

Point Hopping Bucks

— Legend —

Wind Direction

B P C Hunter Stand Location

Hunter Entry Direction

Normal Deer Trails

Point Route Deer Trails

Bucks Hopping From Point to Point

© 2003 Brad Herndon

In the off season, be sure to walk and study every area you hunt in order to determine how big bucks might give you the slip.

Bow sights, quivers, and other parts can loosen up during heavy use. Check all parts for tightness periodically and you won't be disappointed when the moment of truth arrives.

A New—And Bigger—Buck

By the early 1990s, deer were more abundant behind my house, as were the number of hunters who had discovered this public hunting land. Despite this, a new phantom buck had somehow grown up and survived within the region. I had seen his shed antlers and he was a real skyscraper of a 10-point with massive main beams and tines. Yes, I would revisit my old hunting grounds and try those deep saddles once more.

As I did a few years earlier, I hunted the strategic saddles first because they still were the best locations in which to ambush a mature deer. I had good action there, with sightings of does, fawns, small bucks and even a nice mature buck. No big guy showed up. The next step was to check the high trails above the saddles and the point the deer used to avoid me on the hunts I had made years earlier. Surprisingly, nothing of interest showed up in these locations. Then something I had learned about points when hunting a somewhat flat region several years before came into my thoughts.

Deer hunting is a great family sport. Dixie Osborne is shown here with her son, David, and two outstanding bucks they killed. David's buck grosses over 170 inches as a typical while Dixie's 8-point nets 154⅞ inches.

Lowland Points And Their Lessons

The area I was hunting was generally level, as mentioned. However, it was comprised of a long-running, flat plateau which finally dropped off into a large river bottom. Where this plateau ended, a series of small parallel points, much like fingers on a hand, dropped down to the fertile river bottom. Because this drop in elevation was small between the plateau and river plain, the points were short. Each point had a deer trail running along the length of its top, and some deer trails on each of the hillsides. In addition, there were trails going up and down the sides of each point in a perpendicular fashion about halfway down their length. I found this trail fascinating.

Since this region was publicly owned, it had heavy hunting pressure. Most hunters put their time in on stand up on top of the plateau, or if not there, down in the river bottom. This was where the majority of the rubs and scrapes were found, and a maze of heavily rutted trails crisscrossed the terrain. They were the most exciting places to hunt, so therefore the hunters spent their time there. Their success rates, however, were dismal. In this situation, I also noticed how hunters would walk up and down the length of the points to go back and forth between the plateau above and the river bottom below. This is when I came up with my point-hopping theory.

Whitetails love to bed on points. They'll bask in the sun while watching the terrain below and around them for danger. Of course at the same time, they're relying on their noses to alert them to danger. It's a pretty good setup. Since I knew this to be true, I suspected many of the deer were bedding on the sides of these points, or

Because rifles offer extended reach, hunters using them can set up somewhat differently than archers in certain types of terrain configurations.

To avoid working up a sweat walking to your tree stand location, dress lightly and carry extra clothes and other items in a good backpack.

someplace else on them where they couldn't be seen. The people hunting high and low couldn't see them, of course, and if someone walked down the top of the point they were bedded on, the deer could discreetly slip over to the next point to avoid detection.

Thinking my theory was worth a try, one morning I erected my tree stand on one of the finger points near the perpendicular, point-hopping deer trail. The wind was good, my wait was short. Within an hour I had put an arrow through a 3¹⁄₂-year-old 8-pointer that weighed 186 pounds field-dressed. The deer was using the points exactly as I suspected he would.

This lowland point hunt and the point-hopping deer there made me look, once again, at the hilly terrain near my home with an even more discerning eye. I hadn't seen the giant 10-pointer in any of the saddles. It appeared he wasn't using the point between the saddles to avoid me. What was he pulling to keep out of my sight? Getting out the topo map of the region, I studied every aspect of the hills once more. It was then I noticed a terrain feature somewhat similar to my lowland point hunt, only on a larger scale.

Off the east side of the main ridge the hill dropped down steeply, flattened out a smidgen, then forked off into several points which ran parallel to each other. They, in turn, eventually dropped off to the moderately flat section of timber adjoining some farm fields about 2 miles away. This lower section of the hills was chock-full of hunters. The deer sign was good there, plus there was easy walking access to much of the ground.

People hadn't caught on to hunting saddles yet, so the ridgelines carried light human traffic. The occasional hunter, and a few hikers and Boy Scout troops would walk a ridge. This was just enough of a disturbance to keep the whitetails living high on full alert. I outlined a game plan. The next east wind we got I would hunt one of my high-odds saddles. On one of the points I would place a tree stand for Carol to use. She would be able to check to see if the magnum buck was using these points as a survival tool. I put the stand in position where Carol would have a good view, and we waited.

The next east wind blew in on Thanksgiving. Well before daylight, Carol and I walked up a long, steep hill to the main ridge. She dropped off to the east, into the wind, and headed for her stand site, while I walked south to another saddle. Daybreak revealed, as expected, other hunters. Scattered shots rang out randomly east and northeast of me. As the morning progressed, a few deer passed through the saddle before me. At midmorning a shot came from Carol's position. "Maybe she got the monster," I thought.

An hour passed and no Carol. At 11:00 a.m. I met her on the ridgetop before we headed home for our holiday feast. "I missed him!" Carol dejectedly said. "I was watching the points around 9:30 a.m. when I saw movement on one of them. I instantly saw a rack. It was huge. He was angling toward me and at about 70 yards he stopped in some brush. Unfortunately, the east wind switched only slightly and I could tell he immediately winded me. Very slowly he turned around and started to walk back over the point. I had an opening long enough to take one shot. But I missed. Although I checked and checked, I could find no hair or blood. It was a clean miss."

The red arrows in **Illustration 9.3** show how the deer was using the points in a perpendicular fashion to easily avoid me and all the other hunters in this public hunting area. You can also see where Carol had her stand positioned, and where my stand was located in the saddle south of her. We figured out this old buck's little game of avoidance this one time, but never saw him again that hunting season.

One year later, Jeff McElfresh, a friend of mine who lives down the road, called me. "Brad," he said, "I found a dead buck up in the hills behind your house. It looked like it had been dead a couple of days. I cut off the rack and it was so heavy I had to stop a few times and rest when I carried it out. I'll bring it up for you to look at."

It turned out to be the buck Carol had shot at. The 10-pointer was wide and massive. It netted 172 inches as a typical, a somewhat deceptive score. The deer was as bulky in its tines as any rack I have ever seen. It actually had the looks of a 190-inch typical instead of one netting in the low 170s. It was another case of a trophy whitetail that was never tagged by any hunter.

The Hills Are Complex

Many of the hunts I share within this book result in filled tags. In this chapter you've read about two opportunities at trophy deer that resulted in unfilled tags. On one hunt no shot was attempted; the other hunt resulted in a miss. In real life not every hunt is a fairy tale experience. The smarter you get in your hunting plans, however, the more hunts will turn out to be fulfilling.

Moreover, planning hunting strategies with a map is kind of like doing a jigsaw puzzle. It can get mighty frustrating along the way, especially if you think a piece is missing, but it is very satisfying once the picture is complete. The hills, without doubt, comprise one complex puzzle which requires considerable time and study. On the positive side, you already have several of the pieces in place. Now let's grab another one and see where it fits in.

Chapter 10

The Converging Hub
Where Everything Comes Together

The town closest to where I grew up in southern Indiana was Brownstown. Nestled between a range of hills to the south and east and a river bottom to the north and west, it was a cozy setting for about 2,500 residents. As time passed by, a sign was erected on the east edge of town that said, "If You Lived Here You Would Be Home Now." A few years later the words, "The Home Of 2,832 Happy People" were added. As I write this chapter in 2002, Brownstown's population has ballooned to perhaps 3,000 residents.

When I obtained my driver's license in 1959 Brownstown had one stoplight in town, and, by golly, it still has one stoplight.

The stoplight intersection was the place to be. Three restaurants, the library, a drug store, the Royal Theatre and the courthouse all were within half a block of the light. If you sat in this location for any length of time, you would eventually see everyone who was out "cruising".

Yes, the stoplight — the hub — is still the center of activity, just as it's always been. Brownstown was, and still is, a piece of small-town America that makes our nation so great, and so interesting. And fascinatingly, its stoplight and the activity it draws, has a direct tie-in to deer hunting.

Converging Hub Locations

The converging hub can be found in a variety of terrain. And like Brownstown's stoplight, hunting in or near one of these hubs will put you in the middle of excellent deer activity, especially those wild-eyed teenage bucks. Since we've been studying the hills, I'll key in on this type of terrain first.

I previously covered how to discover and hunt inside corners, saddles and hilltop field funnels in the hills. All of these funnels choke deer movement down to a rather tight location and are advantageous to both the archer and firearm hunter. Points and benches have also been discussed, and, overall, they are more difficult to hunt than saddles and hilltop field funnels because of how the wind must be used. Despite this, you read examples of how hunters with either a gun or a bow were able to succeed in these positions. The converging hub is another terrain tool to use while deer hunting. You will find this terrain configuration to be somewhat "loose" in how it pulls deer trails together. Essentially, the deer trails radiate like spokes on a wheel from the center of the hub. But they may not all converge into one precise location. A few of them may combine into one trail passing through the hub, but others will skirt the edges of different terrain

Corn provides a high-energy food source for deer. How deer get to this food source is your key to success. The author had to hunt 3/4 of a mile away from this food source in order to connect on a mature whitetail.

THE CONVERGING HUB

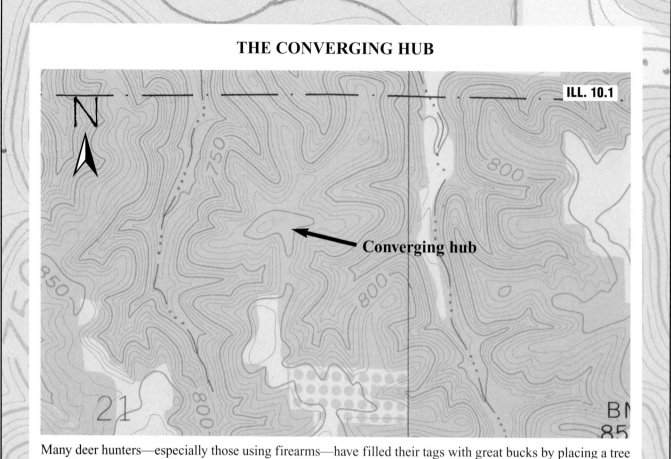

ILL. 10.1

Converging hub

Many deer hunters—especially those using firearms—have filled their tags with great bucks by placing a tree stand in a converging hub.

elements or types of cover. This means, of course, that the firearm hunter will have the highest odds of success when in this stand placement. This doesn't mean the archer can't fill tags in a converging hub. He just has to pick his stand positions more carefully.

Illustration 10.1 is a picture of a topographical map showing moderately hilly terrain. Please pay careful attention to the region where the converging hub arrow is pointed. Notice how the center part of the map has a small stream (meandering blue line with dots) east and west of it, plus one to the north. There are a few small fields in the valley bottoms, and to the south the open area also designates a field. Notice there is one inside corner formed at the northeast corner of this last field that could turn out to be a significant funnel area formed by the terrain. There are also a few hilltop field funnels where creeks head up at this south field. These are stand possibilities. Any of these could be hot stand sites, or

Carol Herndon took this mature 11-point buck by carefully hunting a converging hub. As it often happens, this was the first time she had hunted from this stand location.

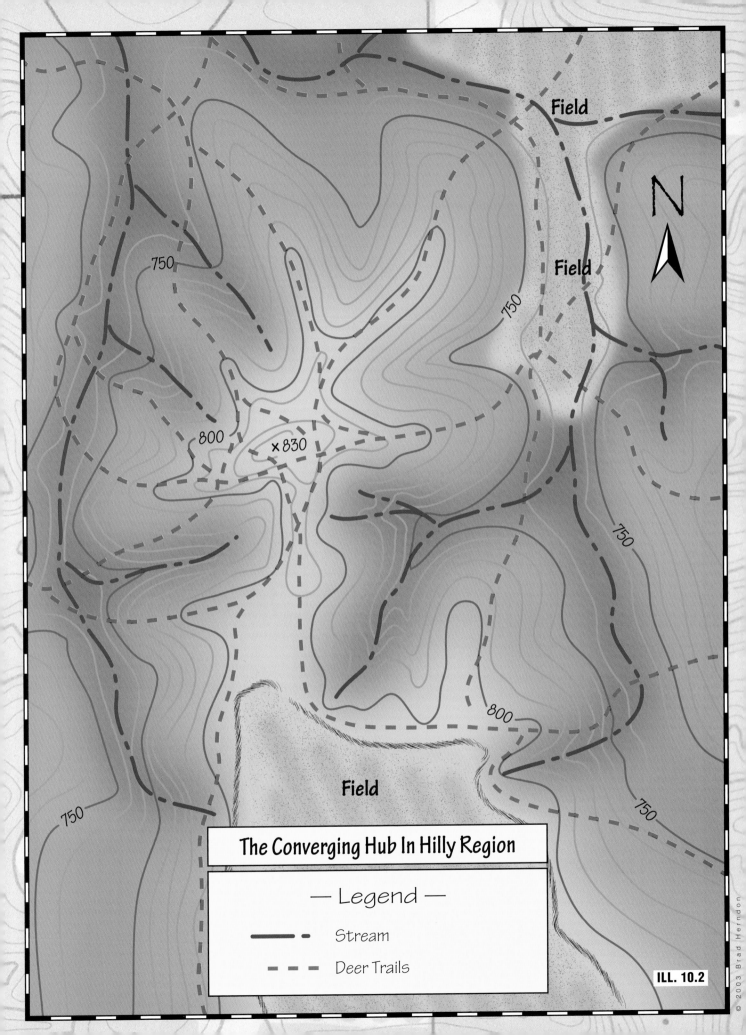

Field

Field

750

750

800

× 830

750

800

750

750

Field

The Converging Hub In Hilly Region

— Legend —

———·— Stream

-------- Deer Trails

ILL. 10.2

© 2003 Brad Herndon

Rory Cowles is an early-season big buck specialist. This excellent 10-point netted 144-4/8 inches and was taken by hunting the outer edge of a converging hub that contained a quantity of white oak trees that were dropping acorns.

none of them could be. This is true because this field is remote and hidden from any road, so deer may feel comfortable crossing the field during daylight hours, thereby unknowingly avoiding your tree stand placement.

In other words, this forested region may very well hold several deer, and some good ones, but other than the inside corner and hilltop field funnels, it is, at first glance, difficult to hunt. Going back to the converging hub arrow, consider how the terrain is arranged. There are actually six points of various sizes and shapes running up to the center of this hub, plus the ridgeline from the south. Some points are large and lengthy, while some are short and small. Moreover, all are significant since they can carry whitetail traffic into the center of the hub. This is the type of converging hub you are looking for when you are poring over topographical maps of hilly sections. Once these hubs of activity are discovered, then scouting the site, if possible, will determine where the deer trails are located, and how they might best be hunted.

To show you what the deer trails in the hilly terrain shown in **Illustration 10.1** might look like, I have added a drawing, **Illustration 10.2**, for illustrative purposes. I have purposely made my drawing of the topo map shown in **Illustration 10.1** very simple, leaving out a few contour lines so I would have room to draw in the deer trails. Another thing I have done with this map is to leave out where the hunter's best stand site might be, what wind direction would need to be used to hunt a specific location, and how the hunter would get into, and out of, his stand. In other words, I'm leaving you on your own to a large degree on this one, since when you study a topo map, you are eventually going to have to figure these locations and strategies out on your own.

As you look this drawing over, consider what spots might be best for a stand site and what wind directions you would need to hunt these positions. As always, using the wind wisely is critical to your success. Be sure to pick a low impact entry route to your stand. Take your time as

you look at the map. There's no hurry. You should be able to recognize the inside corner on the map in the northeast corner of the south field, and you will also notice the hilltop field funnels formed around the perimeter of the field. These could be productive, as mentioned earlier. However, from all appearances the deer trails where all the points and the ridgetop come together is the hub and should be the real hot spot.

Where all the deer trails loosely converge at the hub is high ground and enables you to use the wind wisely. Oak trees may also be located in this area and can produce good hunting early in the year, and even late in the season if the acorns are plentiful. And for those of you who enjoy sitting a strategic position with scrapes and rubs nearby, the converging hub oftentimes has both in abundance. A smart bow hunter can tap out a nice buck in such a location if he hunts a scrape during the pre-rut when bucks are still using them.

If you have hung tough with me to this stage of the book in your quest for hunting knowledge, you should have a stand site or two picked out by now on **Illustration 10.2**. I like the location just east of the figure showing 830 feet elevation on the map.

Whitetails love to eat acorns. You can take some high-scoring early-season bucks if you can locate a funnel the deer pass through while on their way to this nutritious food source.

Many hunters put in for public land draw hunts in terrain they're unfamiliar with. Topographical maps can quickly reveal bottlenecks the whitetails will naturally use when avoiding other hunters.

I would enter my stand site by coming up the creek to the east of this position. Once on top I could use a northwest wind to hunt the converging hub. By hunting this way I would have walked over very few deer trails while coming in, and the northwest wind would carry my scent to very few places where deer would normally walk. By hunting during firearms season, a hunter in this position should get a crack at most deer using the converging hub.

If this is one of the places you picked to place a stand, then you're well on your way to being a true map hunter. You probably, at this time, are also able to assemble in your mind what the terrain looks like when studying the contour elevations on topographical maps. When you reach this level of map reading, you will find using topo maps to be invaluable for speed scouting new regions. I'll share an example of how this works.

Public Land Draw Hunts

Many of you may put in for drawings so you can hunt public land such as state parks, refuges, or military reservations. Normally these protected sites hold high numbers of whitetails, plus some real wall-hangers. On one hunt at a military reservation a few years back, I sat in a building waiting for my assigned hunting area to be revealed to me. About an hour before daylight, I found out I would be hunting in a hilly region in the northern part of the reserve. Whipping out the topo maps I had of the entire region, I pored over my assigned area. Within minutes I noticed a hilly hub similar to the one I've just discussed. A portable battery powered weather radio I carried revealed a north wind was to continue all day.

At daylight, I eased up a creek along the south side of the hub. By reading the topo map I could tell where I was walking in relation to terrain features nearby. Reaching the spot below the hub, I slipped up to the top of the hill and took my stand. Within two hours I had a 4½-year old 8-pointer on the ground. What's tremendously interesting about this hunt is

When bucks cross fields they are often traveling from one flat land hub to another.

the fact I had never been in this region before in my life! The recounting of this memorable hunt drives home the importance of what the study of a topographical map and the use of a weather radio can do. Without them, I would have been wandering around all day, stinking up the region as I searched for the key location.

As noted, on this particular hunt I used a creek below the hub as my approach. Most of the time, you should find this to be the most advantageous entry to a hilly hub stand site. Other times, a little-used ridge or point may be the best approach. This part of hub hunting should be studied by walking the region in the off-season if possible.

Flat Hubs Are Often Overlooked

Funnels, funnels, funnels. As you've read, I preach about finding these narrow deer passageways because they are so important to filling your deer tag every year. And many observant whitetail enthusiasts have picked up on recognizing these prime positions, especially on

level land. This is because it is relatively easy to see them while in the field, on topographical maps, and even on aerial maps. As this book has revealed, these flatland funnels may be inside corners, double inside corners, deer trails running along rivers or small streams, or heavy fencerows connecting two woodlots. While all these locations can be awesome, at times indiscreet terrain features can be overlooked which may increase your chances of success even more.

As an illustration, let me use some hunts my wife Carol and I have made over the years in Illinois. The Prairie State is most often thought of as a farm state chock-full of nothing but farm fields, primarily corn and soybeans, with its flat, rich soil being some of the most fertile ground on earth. This is the case for the most part although there are vast sections of hills in the southern part of the state, and other smaller hilly regions in some other parts of Illinois. That Illinois grows quantities of monstrous bucks is com-

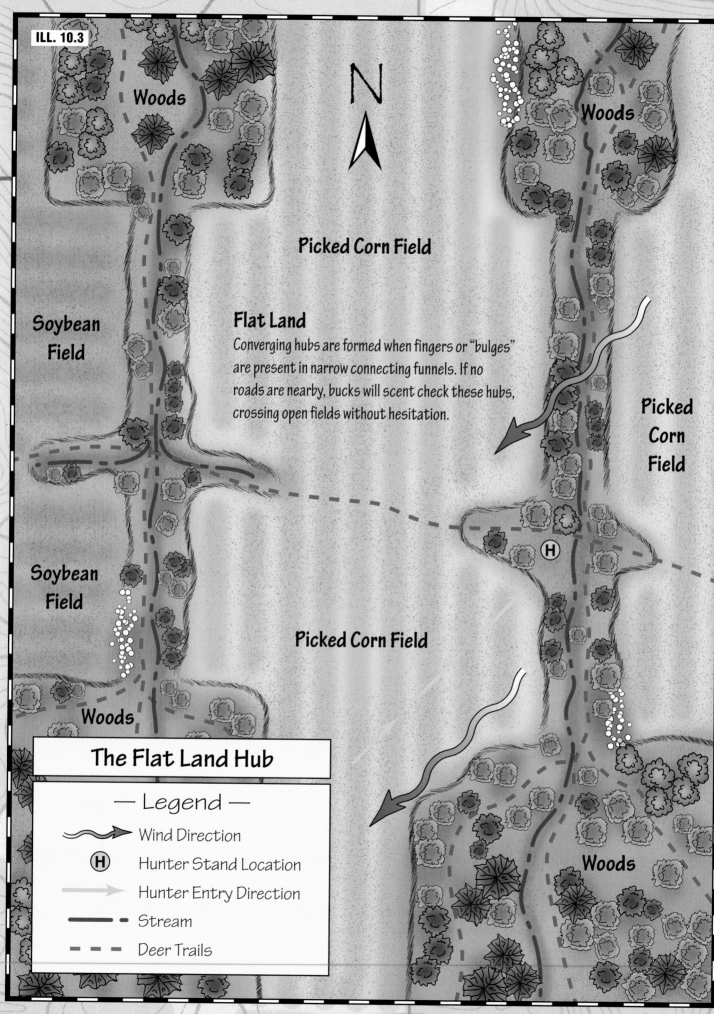

ILL. 10.3

N

Woods

Woods

Picked Corn Field

Soybean Field

Flat Land
Converging hubs are formed when fingers or "bulges" are present in narrow connecting funnels. If no roads are nearby, bucks will scent check these hubs, crossing open fields without hesitation.

Picked Corn Field

Ⓗ

Soybean Field

Picked Corn Field

Woods

Woods

The Flat Land Hub

— Legend —

Wind Direction

Ⓗ Hunter Stand Location

Hunter Entry Direction

Stream

Deer Trails

© 2003 Brad Herndon

mon knowledge. These brutish whitetails draw many non-resident hunters to Illinois, Carol and I included.

As we hunted Illinois over the years, we found several of the key ambush placements previously mentioned. As time went on, however, we picked up on the fact deer crossed open fields quite frequently. This was especially true of any fields hidden from the roads. Further study of these locations uncovered several interesting facts.

First of all, if thin timber bordering small streams in farm country has "bulges" in it, deer will at times cross fields at these points. One of these bulges most often is formed when a small ditch draining a field joins the bigger stream. At times, two small drainages may come into a bigger stream at the same general location, one on each side. These small drainages oftentimes have trees or brush near where they join the larger stream, essentially forming a small hub. This is very discreet and somewhat hard to understand so a detailed drawing is shown in **Illustration 10.3** of this often overlooked terrain feature.

What Makes A Flat Hub Great

During the rut, bucks are out covering ground. We know that, and this is why we position ourselves in a narrow funnel connecting two large tracts of cover. I did this in Illinois and had success, counting on bucks running the length of these long, narrow funnels while checking for receptive does. Interestingly, one region I hunted had three narrow funnels formed by the brush along streams. Each lay parallel to the other about ¼ to ½ mile apart.

This is one area where I noticed deer crossing fields a lot, going from one funnel to another, but not always traveling their length. This made sense to me as I thought about it. Instead of going the length of an entire funnel, which may be a mile or more, to search for a hot doe, the bucks could hit each funnel crossways at the hub, check for scent on the main trail, then hightail it over to the next funnel region if they wanted to. This saved them time as they made their rounds.

Being an experimenter, I decided to abandon my narrow spots in the funnels for a while and try these miniature hubs to see if things panned out. This was a gamble since I was bowhunting, making the wind harder to use, entry and exit to stand more difficult, and could put more deer out of my limited shooting range.

The investment of time was worthwhile. On one of my first hunts in one crossover hub, I killed a 4½-year-old buck that weighed 202 pounds field-dressed. While waiting to track this buck, a borderline Pope & Young buck came traipsing by. Other miniature hubs like this have proved rewarding as well. I've seen as many as eight bucks

during one hunt in one of these hubs. That's not bad.

I have discovered these flatland hubs while hunting deer in Illinois, Iowa, and Indiana. While in the south turkey hunting I have seen similarly constructed flatland hubs. Incidentally, these hubs can be found in both crop-farming country and pastureland areas. In addition to what I have shared thus far, look for any narrow funnel region where it bends toward woods, or where the point of a forested tract comes out toward the funnel. These are natural crossing places for all whitetails because it's the shortest distance across the field.

Flatland hubs may also be formed where two brushy fencerows cross, where two different power lines, gas lines or something of that nature cross in a woods, or even where logging roads meet. Don't forget to look for low spots in fields or pastures since these low spots allow deer to stay out of sight when roads are nearby, allowing them to move undetected from one piece of cover to another. All of these types of terrain can form great converging hubs. Don't overlook any of them.

And although this book doesn't cover Quality Deer Management, I do want to mention one intriguing way you can create your own converging hub if you own land and can plant food plots of substantial size.

I once ran into a landowner (he will go unnamed) who was very sharp when it came to manipulating deer movement. He was a hunter who owned a large tract of basically flat ground, and was into planting food plots for the whitetails on his property. The entire region was grown up fields, brush or hardwoods, with no terrain features such as creeks or hills to funnel the deer into any one particular location. He told me he knew food plots would help him to some degree since it would pull deer to a specific location, but because they could meander wherever they wanted to, it wouldn't help him a significant amount when it came to killing them.

Four years ago he came up with a novel idea. In the center of his property where most of the grown up fields and brush was located, he constructed six food plots in a hub design. Each was very narrow, but very long. From the air it looked like the spokes of a giant wheel going into a central hub. While the deer still could come and go wherever they wanted to, their tendency as they fed in the food plots was to follow the narrow length of the fields. This, of course, led many of the whitetails, including bucks, right through the center of the hub. This land manager has two strategically placed shooting houses located there, and they have produced well for him. It was good thinking on his part.

As usual, good thinking pays off. As you study your maps and walk the regions you hunt be sure to always be on the lookout for converging hubs. They are, after all, where everything comes together.

Chapter 11
Hunting Breakline
Bucks

Carol Herndon took
her first archery buck
by hunting a breakline
in an 80-acre woods.

Put on your most comfortable walking boots. Inside corners, perfect funnels, and saddles in the hills are all easily found once a hunter becomes experienced at reading a topographical map. This is not so with breaklines. They require legwork.

Breaklines are most often formed when one section of a wood is logged, while the rest of the timber is left alone. In just a few years, this leaves one part of the wood thick and brushy, while the other region is more open. The line where these two different types of cover meet is what I call a breakline. Breaklines will be found in flat and hilly terrain, and, when hunted correctly, will consistently produce deer. Whitetails, especially bucks, will "hold" to almost any breakline.

The topographical map, my favorite tool for locating "deer traps," will never reveal a breakline. The topo map shows terrain features such as elevations, streams, lakes, and other pertinent information, but it can't show timber harvests. The aerial map, if studied carefully, can be helpful in finding breaklines. This is true because the aerial photograph will show the details of brush and mature timber, which are somewhat different in appearance. If you really know what you are looking for, you will be able to discover a breakline by studying an aerial map. Despite this, breaklines are most often uncovered by observant hunters who put in lots of miles in the woods.

In addition to my deer hunting outings, I've found breaklines while I've been mushroom, turkey, squirrel, and grouse hunting. The more outdoor hobbies you have, the more opportunities you have to come across these strategic terrain features. Once you find a breakline, analyze what you see very carefully, since this will enable you to intelligently hunt the area. And keep in mind a breakline can be productive for many years. In 1980 my fourth bow-kill, an 11-point 2½-year-old buck, came from a breakline. Six years later Carol got her first bow-kill, a yearling buck, by hunting from the same tree I did in 1980. She also made the same entry to her tree stand that I did, and was using the same wind directions.

In **Illustration 11.1** the drawing shows exactly how this breakline is laid out in the woods where we harvested those two deer. It shows details of how deer use this forested tract, and how we hunted it. Incidentally, this particular breakline is located in level ground, so I'll cover flatland breaklines first.

The region where Carol and I killed the two bucks contained a woods-related breakline, one I had discovered back in 1980 when I killed the 11-point buck. The woods where this hunt occurred was a flat 80-acre woods in a huge river bottom area. For several decades the timber in this woods was allowed to grow, reaching near-virgin timber proportions. Then, in 1974, the landowner decided to start harvesting the timber, selectively cutting

A fast way to find breaklines in the timber is to talk to loggers. Grouse, rabbit, and raccoon hunters can often tip you off to these hot spots as well.

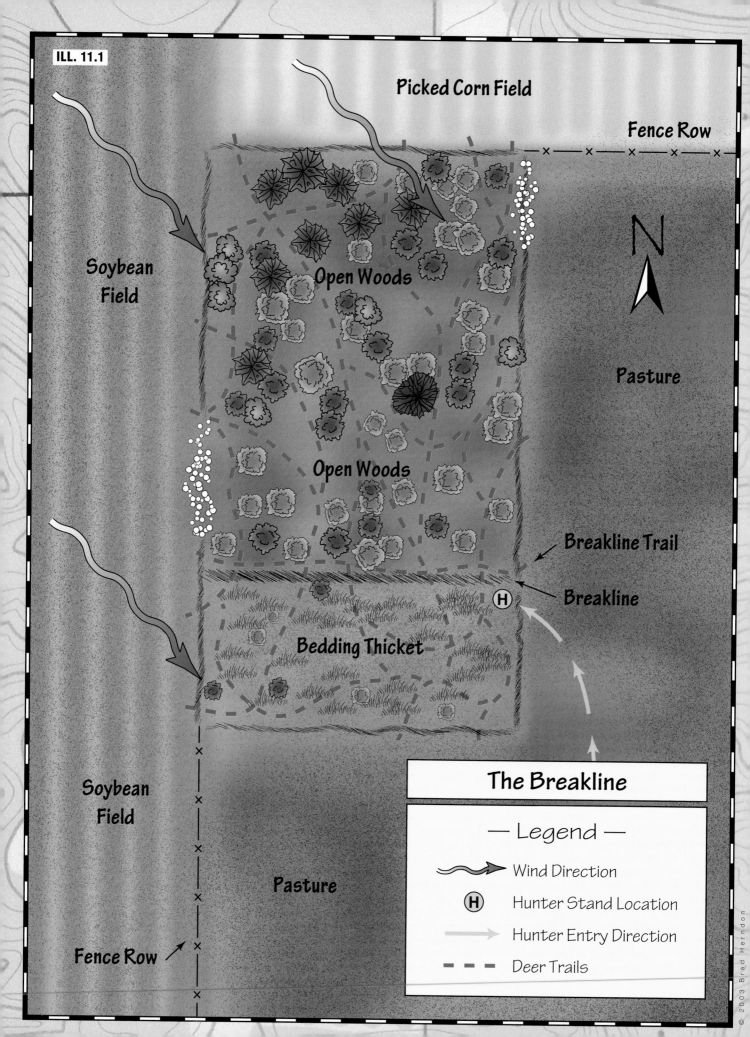

ILL. 11.1

Picked Corn Field

Fence Row

Soybean
Field

Open Woods

Pasture

Open Woods

Breakline Trail

Breakline

Bedding Thicket

H

Soybean
Field

Pasture

Fence Row

The Breakline

— Legend —

Wind Direction

H Hunter Stand Location

Hunter Entry Direction

Deer Trails

© 2003 Brad Herndon

Find a good breakline in a timbered area and you have discovered an excellent location in which to kill deer of all sizes, including some buster bucks.

20 acres in the south end first. Later, in 15-year intervals, he would continue this well-managed harvest.

When I walked the woods in 1980, the south end had experienced a dramatic facelift. Instead of a woods dotted with beautiful and massive white oaks, sweet gum, hickories, maple and various other hardwood species, the south end was a regular thicket. Small hardwood trees 6 to 12 inches in diameter had been left to grow for future harvesting but the woods was for the most part a jungle of small saplings and grapevines. A human almost had to crawl through the entanglement. Deer, however, loved it. The brush provided excellent forage for them and a perfect bedding grounds.

The section of the woods where the thicket met the mature timber formed the breakline. Deer used this breakline in two manners. First, they traveled perpendicular to the breakline, meandering in and out of the breakline in various places. They also traveled parallel to the breakline. A trail ran the length of the breakline, located in the open section of woods where walking was easy. This trail varied in its distance from the thicket

Pay attention to details; especially when bow hunting. Be sure to trim out shooting lanes to assure you get a clear shot at that buck of a lifetime when he comes waltzing by your tree stand.

edge, but stayed between 5 feet and 5 yards from the thicket.

Obviously, a deer could have been killed on any of these trails, although a hunter's luck would need to be running good when hunting from some positions. Consider the trails running perpendicular to the break-line. Commonly, on a breakline of any length in flat land, several of these trails will be evident. Some are used more frequently than others by the deer, but none experience exclusive use. Deer may come out on one, and then go back in the thicket on another. I have seen them loop in and out on several trails during a morning period.

So while you may pick a perpendicular trail and the winds of fate blow favorably on you, allowing a buck to amble by, don't count on this happening often. For an example, let's consider hunting a trail crossing the breakline near the middle of the woods. To get to our stand position, we would have to walk through one half of the woods. This stinks up 50 percent of the woods with our scent, alerting deer traveling in that region to our presence.

When hunting this position, the wind should ideally be blowing your scent back in the direction from which you entered. This leaves you at least one half of the woods where deer aren't aware you have invaded their domain. Do you like 50-50 odds, though? I don't, and

neither should you. A 50 percent chance of success, by the way, is the highest your odds will be from this stand location. Some antsy hunters who can not wait for the correct wind will walk to the stand with the wind to their back, cross the deer trail so they will be downwind of it, then erect their stand. This means the hunter has walked through one half of the woods, with scent spewing into the other half. That hunter is now banking on a deer leaving or entering the cutover on just one of the many trails available. And even if that happens, the hunter must shoot the deer before it comes to the point where he walked across the trail! Hunting in this way creates poor odds of success and should be avoided.

There are far better hunting methods to utilize when hunting woods-related breaklines. They are time-proven (I have been studying and hunting breaklines since 1975) and work equally well in all parts of the country.

As you will notice in **Illustration 11.1**, the area we were hunting was a rectangular shape, with its length running north and south. Five trails are marked that cross perpendicular to the breakline. The deer used these trails to enter or leave the thicket. In past years I observed deer using these types of trails, sometimes coming out of the thicket on one trail, browsing on acorns a little, and then looping back into the thicket on another trail.

Brad and Carol Herndon live in a little log home in the edge of the hills in southern Indiana, not far from where Brad was raised.

Outstanding bucks can be taken from breaklines found in both hilly and flat regions.

The key to success in this situation is to disregard all the perpendicular trails except the outermost perpendicular trails, keying instead on the trail traveling along the length of the breakline. My years of observation have shown that sometime during most days, bucks will travel this parallel breakline trail. It provides open, easy walking from one side of the woods to the other, and in addition, as a buck crosses each perpendicular trail entering the thicket, he can scent-check them for a doe in estrus. The breakline trail, running close to the brushy undergrowth, also is an excellent location for bucks to place scrapes and rubs.

In the woods Carol and I hunted, the farthest east perpendicular trail showed considerably less deer sign than trails nearer the center of the woods. This is where patience and confidence enter in. I knew sooner or later, if hunting with the perfect wind, a buck would wander up the breakline, presenting a perfect shot. Of course, on our hunts we had to be patient, waiting for the correct wind and then being very careful in our approach to stand.

In this particular case, deer fed within the woods quite a little bit, plus in fields to the north and west. By circling and entering from the southeast, we were able to slip in with the deer unaware we were ever there, except if they strayed into the southeast corner sometime later in the night.

As you can see by our entry and the wind direction, we had fully utilized and stacked every advantage in our favor by using a northwest wind and walking in a very small portion of the woods. On Carol's hunt, once she was on stand, she had an almost unbelievable thing happen. A buck came along only five minutes later and she drilled it! Although Carol was fortunate a buck showed up so soon, it certainly came as no surprise to me that she was successful from that particular spot. When I killed the buck in 1980, I had made the exact same entry and also was hunting with a northwest wind. Who says lightning doesn't strike in the same place twice!

I feel I could have taken other bucks from this breakline over the past few years, but trophy hunting has prevented me from doing so. The area is hunted heavily during the gun season, keeping the antlered bucks in the 1½- or 2½-year-old age class. As a result, I make only an occasional hunt there, and then merely to check for signs of trophy whitetails.

Breaklines In The Hills

In 1986 I was hunting a large hilly region of public land consisting of approximately 2,000 acres. Deer were scarce there, but of the few residing in the hardwood hills, a few were of whopper proportions. It was tough hunting, though, because no strategic, can't miss, ambush features could be found in the geography of the land.

One day while musing over the dilemma, I considered one brushy region of the hills where a timber harvest had been conducted five years previously. Of course a breakline was formed where the brush and open timber met. Even though this locale held very few deer, the breakline was interesting from the standpoint that it connected other parts of the hills where family units of deer lived. Examination of the breakline proved to be intriguing. Absolutely no trails criss-crossed the breakline. One faint trail in the open woods paralleled the breakline, nothing else.

Still, the area held potential. I suspected the breakline trail could be used by big bucks when going from one family unit to another in hopes of finding a hot doe. The setup seemed too easy to be true. The breakline trail was even down at the base of the hills where it was flat for a considerable distance, meaning the wind would not switch directions there. All I had to do was wait for a wind crossing the trail, sneak in from the downwind side, and a buck would never know I was there.

The first week of November I decided to invest a few days testing my strategy. On the fourth hunt I arrowed a 3½-year-old 8-pointer that weighed 178 pounds after it was field dressed. Once again a buck, a breakline and a bow hunter had all came together at the same time.

Bucks of all sizes relate to, and use, breaklines in some manner. The open woods is an ideal location for them to place scrapes and rubs.

You will find similar breaklines in the hills, and as you can see from this example, this particular breakline was used somewhat differently by the deer than most of the ones found in level land. The deer didn't move in a perpendicular fashion across this breakline. In essence, each breakline has to be walked and studied to see how whitetails use it. In the hills, the lay of the land will often determine where you can hunt, and where you can't. This is because of the way the wind washes over the curving and projecting terrain. And, yes, I know you may get tired of me harping about being careful of the wind in hilly regions. But, the truth is, wind will cause you an extreme amount of grief if you hunt carelessly.

Women catch on to deer hunting fast when they have an experienced hunter assisting them. Kelly Reynolds poses with her husband, Henry, and a fine buck she took during the 2000 season.

Look For The Unusual Breakline

I have one other significant comment regarding breaklines. While breaklines created by logging operations are the ones most often discovered in a woods, it is noteworthy to mention that *every* geographical feature of your hunting area should be carefully checked.

In 1987, John Johnson and a friend were scouting in late bow season near Bedford, Indiana. They were walking in a woods that dropped down from a slightly elevated section of hills to join the bank of the White River. When they tired of walking, they started back down to the river where they had left their boat. About 100 yards from the river, a steep limestone bluff nearly 9 feet high ran the length of the woods. As luck would have it, John and his friend stopped for a breather on top of the limestone ledge.

It was then they noticed a faint deer trail running along the base of the ledge. Almost at the same time, movement in the horseweeds 25 yards down the trail drew their attention. It was a huge buck coming right by

them! John barely had time to draw and shoot (his friend had left his bow at home since they were only scouting). A spine shot dropped the buck in his tracks.

The non-typical was incredible! It had 14-points, including two beautiful drop tines. To accentuate its beautiful antlers, the buck had a field-dressed weight — and this is not a typo — of 307 pounds! The buck scored 196 6/8 Pope & Young points and held the Indiana non-typical archery kill record for a time, although it has since been displaced.

I'm sure you noticed this awesome buck, just like bucks smaller in stature, was relating to, and traveling along, a breakline. Breaklines of various configurations may be found in all sorts of whitetail habitat. It is up to you, the terrain strategist, to be confident and observant. The "secrets" are out there just waiting to be discovered.

Many book whitetails survive by holing up in fencerows and ditches during hunting seasons.

Chapter 12

Hunting
Fencerow
Phantoms

The topography on the North American continent where whitetail enthusiasts can pursue their sport runs the gamut, from swamps to mountaintops. Moreover, though, the majority of land where hunters spend their time is moderately hilly, gently rolling, or flat land. Almost all deer hunters agree the hills are the most difficult to hunt, both from a physical and strategic standpoint. So where it is available, gently rolling or flat ground, interspersed with woodlots, is the favored terrain in which to search for a monster buck. Better yet, little effort is required to get to the many funnels found in these level regions, and the wind is easy to use to the hunter's advantage.

With this being said, there is one type of flat-land hunting that may be as intimidating to a deer hunter as even the steeper hills: Flat, open stretches of farm or ranch land, stretching for miles on end, with only a few woodlots, fencerows, ditches and small streams criss-crossing the region. "The deer just bed in the fencerows, or the middle of the fields," a hunter may say, "and it's impossible to kill them, especially after a day or two of hunting pressure."

In this situation, hunters may try driving the deer out of woodlots, but the whitetails in the timber simply head off cross-country, rarely presenting a shot to the standers.

Other hunters, meanwhile, take stands in the nearest woods to the region, hoping the big bucks will "circle through" while looking for a receptive doe. This often doesn't work because so many tree stand hunters spend time in the few tracts of timber available that the older deer avoid these locations during daylight hours. So as a result of this difficulty, many mature whitetails go on, year after year, adding inches to already impressive antlers. Illinois, Iowa and Kansas are classic examples of states where this frequently happens.

Interestingly, in reports I have had from Illinois, hunters have told me some of the biggest bucks will bed in the middle of a picked corn field. There a few weeds will give them the slightest amount of cover. These same hunters tell me the deer are extremely hard to see in these fields unless you have sharp eyes, use quality binoculars, and are positioned high so you can look down into the field, rather than across it. Of course this is hard to do in totally flat land. Many Illinois' hunters believe these ancient bucks will actually spend their daylight hours in these fields during the intense hunting pressure found during Illinois' short three-day November firearm season.

While these fencerow phantoms drive many a frustrated hunter to abandon a vast, open area entirely, it's not true for a similar section of northern Indiana where

Steve Knebel is the master of the fencerows.

Steve Knebel lives. I know of no man who is better at hunting fencerows and ditches then Knebel, and I believe what you can learn from his hunting methods will be substantial. He is what I call The Fencerow Master.

The Credentials

My wife Carol and I met Steve Knebel 12 years ago at the Hoosier Deer Classic in Indianapolis, Indiana. We immediately were taken with his friendliness, his quick smile, and his upbeat, optimistic attitude. His being a whitetail fanatic sealed our friendship. And while we could see he was in the initial stages of learning how to hunt mature bucks, it was obvious he was going to get better, much better, at the deer hunting game. Consider what he has accomplished over the last 10 years:

a) His top three typical whitetails average 158 gross, 143 net. His top six typical bucks average 148 $^4/_8$ inches gross, 136 net.

b) Average field-dressed weight of his three heaviest deer is 215 pounds. His six heaviest average 204 pounds field-dressed. His biggest deer is a bulky 12-pointer, 163 $^2/_8$ inch gross bow kill that tipped the scales to 233 pounds!

c) His last nine bucks taken with a firearm all were taken by stalking.

Keep in mind here the definition of stalking. Still-hunting is where you slip along, hoping to see a deer and shoot it. Most of the time a still-hunter has the whitetails move into him as he eases along. Stalking, on the other hand, is deer hunting's most difficult method of attaining success. You actually see the buck before he sees you, often when he's bedded, then stalk up to within shooting range, undetected. Have you ever pulled this feat off, even one time? Can you imagine doing this nine consecutive times? I can't. That's why this chapter revolves around the terrain strategies Knebel uses in flat land, and how he uses fencerows and ditches to pull off his difficult, but successful hunts.

As you read this, keep in mind that his success is even more amazing considering the fact Knebel has accomplished all this in a state where trophy deer management is not a priority, and where a long 16-day firearm season in the middle of the rut keeps antlered deer cropped down closely. In addition, Indiana has a 16-day muzzle-loader season in December. How does he do it? I'll turn him loose to explain his methods, for he has done a masterful job of sharing in one chapter what it has taken him years to learn.

Finding Fencerow Phantoms

"I keep in touch with a lot of landowners year-round," said Knebel. "They tip me off to any big bucks on their property. And while I do watch for nice bucks in late summer to some degree, it's not as much as some people might think. Actually, here in northern Indiana I keep track of the late winter yarding groups, and it tells me how many whitetails of the size I am interested in harvesting survived.

"My terrain up here is mostly flat farmland, dotted with woods," Knebel notes. "On average, 10 percent of a square mile (a square mile is 640 acres) might be woods. There usually are a few fencerows and ditches intersecting the land, but some of this ground up here is mostly wide-open fields. You guys down south, where there are lots of woods, would probably make fun of me for hunting some places I do.

"As fall progresses, I keep close track of the farm harvest, especially the cornfields," Knebel emphasized.

"When it's available, I really like to hunt around standing corn because I feel that's where the big bucks hang out. They are there because it provides security from the firearm hunters, plus cornfields are loaded with does, or at least have a hot doe in there. I like to hunt the edges of woods bordering standing cornfields so I can look down into the corn. These woods edges and fencerows are my favorite places to hunt. My heaviest deer, a 12-point bow kill that field-dressed 233 pounds, was taken from a stand situated along a woods edge adjoining a standing cornfield.

"The last nine bucks I have taken during firearms season all have been taken by stalking," Knebel added. "This doesn't mean I don't spend time in a tree stand during shotgun season when the rut is going strong. Usually early in the morning I will spend time in a tree. This may be in a stand I already have set up from bow season, or it may mean I put a couple of steps in a single tree out in a field or ditch. The whole point here is to get me high so I can watch 300, 400 or more acres. When it gets daylight, I may see a buck, or two bucks hanging around a doe out in an open field. Sometimes they go off out of sight. Other times they bed in a fencerow or ditch.

If the buck is a shooter, then I formulate a plan and go after him. Most of the time I'm familiar with the region, but maps can sure help you out at times, refreshing your memory as to how all the fencerows, ditches and woods are put together and how deer might use them."

Making The Stalk

"The first thing I have to determine," said Knebel, "is whether I have permission to go on the ground where the deer bedded down. Memory and plat maps help me in this respect. If I have permission, then I study the wind direction. Most of the time deer will bed on the downwind side of a fencerow, even if the fencerow has little cover. It is always best to have a headwind or crosswind of some kind to stalk a bedded deer. Stalking bedded deer when there is no wind at all is very difficult, but it can be done.

"Nine times out of 10, during the rut a buck *will not* be bedded alone along a fencerow or ditch bank," Knebel remarked. "A buck is usually with a doe. Take some time before the stalk to try locating the other deer. How far

Most tree stand injuries occur as deer hunters are climbing or descending the tree. Always be extremely careful.

from the buck is she? On which side of him is she bedded? And, **which way is she looking**. If you don't analyze the situation somewhat, the doe could pick you off before you ever get close enough for a shot at the buck. Good binoculars in the 7- to 10-power range, or even a spotting scope, help at this time.

"There's one other thing to watch for," cautions Knebel. "Before starting a stalk, pick out landmarks in relation to where the deer are bedded, such as bushes, trees, rock piles, etc. If none exist, such as in a clean fencerow, try counting fence posts to keep track of exactly where the deer are. A few feet one way or another might make a big difference in whether or not you fill that tag."

Knebel also mentioned to me how important confidence is in pulling off a successful stalk. He is a very humble person, by the way, and certainly doesn't want to come off as sounding the least bit arrogant. Still, confidence is a key to filling your tag in this electrifying manner. Knebel noted you must have confidence in getting up on the deer, and even greater confidence in being mentally prepared for what is going to happen in the next 30 seconds or so once you are in shooting position. Incidentally, Knebel gets up on approximately 90 percent of the bucks

he finds bedded, noting that if he sees a buck bedded in a fencerow, he thinks he is going to get him.

As might be expected, the stalk usually is made in a slow, extremely observant manner, although if the cover is excellent you can move fairly quickly. Normally though, available cover will dictate a slow walk, or even a belly crawl at times. Usually the stalk is made on the opposite side of the fencerow the deer is bedded in. This gives you the cover you need, and the wind Knebel previously mentioned helps muffle your steps in the picked corn or soybean field. The wind also is rustling around weeds or corn stalks, and this movement helps conceal your movements. Finally, all of this confidence, keen observance of the deer's position, and careful stalking will bring you to within shooting distance of the trophy whitetail. A shot, incidentally, that may be a lot closer than you might expect.

The Shot

"When you get into your final position for the shot," Knebel said, "sometimes you have to do something to get the buck to stand up for a better shot. Grunting, tossing stones or corn cobs, breaking sticks, or even shaking the fence all work for me. This really gets your heart pumping. Usually when a buck jumps up in a fencerow, he'll trot out to about 40 to 50 yards, then sometimes — but not always — stop to look back, offering a good shot. If he gets out to 40 or 50 yards and doesn't look like he is going to stop, you had better be taking the shot, provided you have a good angle on the deer.

"I have shot most of my big deer from fencerows and ditch banks before they get 25 or 30 yards out," Knebel added. "I'm not taking any chances on him not stopping to look back.

"When hunting ditch banks," he continued, "be extra alert if the stalk is made on the same side of the ditch that the buck is bedded. Most likely in this case the buck will go charging up the opposite bank from you, so be prepared to shoot fast in this situation. My 1994 deer that had a total gross score of 170 inches, and my 1995 deer, grossing over 154 inches, both did just that — went racing up the opposite bank. Be prepared!"

Maps Show How It's Done

As the old saying goes, a picture is worth 1,000 words. This being true, two maps showing how Knebel pulled off successful stalks on trophy bucks are included with this chapter. **Illustration 12.1** shows his route when he tagged a dandy 10-point buck in 1993. Note how

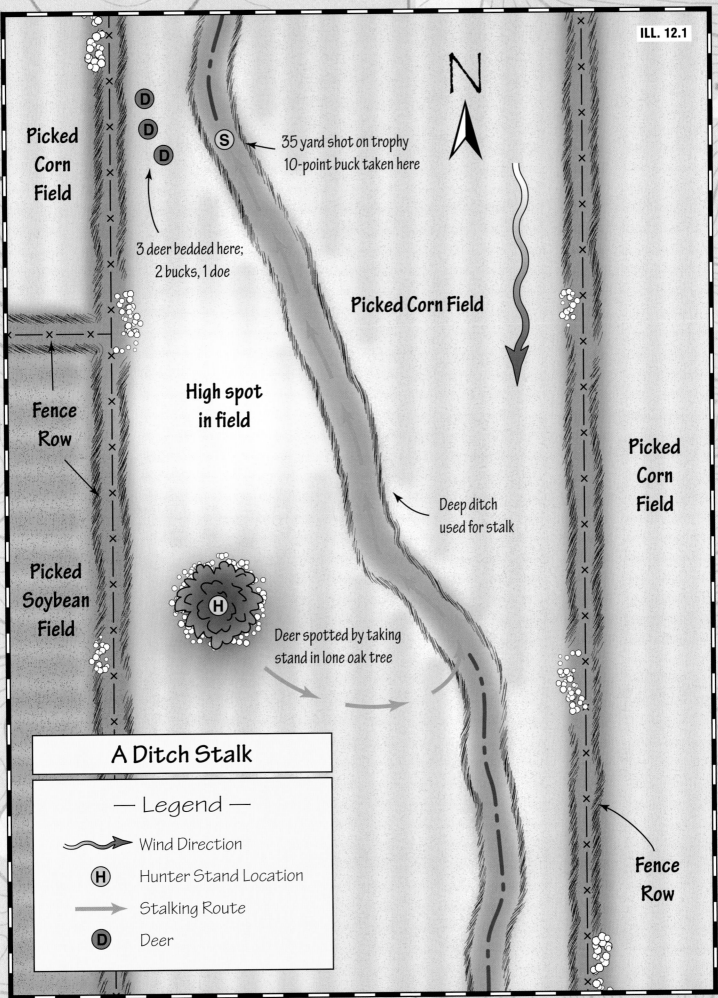

ILL. 12.1

Picked Corn Field

35 yard shot on trophy 10-point buck taken here

3 deer bedded here; 2 bucks, 1 doe

Picked Corn Field

High spot in field

Fence Row

Deep ditch used for stalk

Picked Corn Field

Picked Soybean Field

Deer spotted by taking stand in lone oak tree

A Ditch Stalk

— Legend —

Wind Direction

(H) Hunter Stand Location

Stalking Route

(D) Deer

Fence Row

© 2003 Brad Herndon

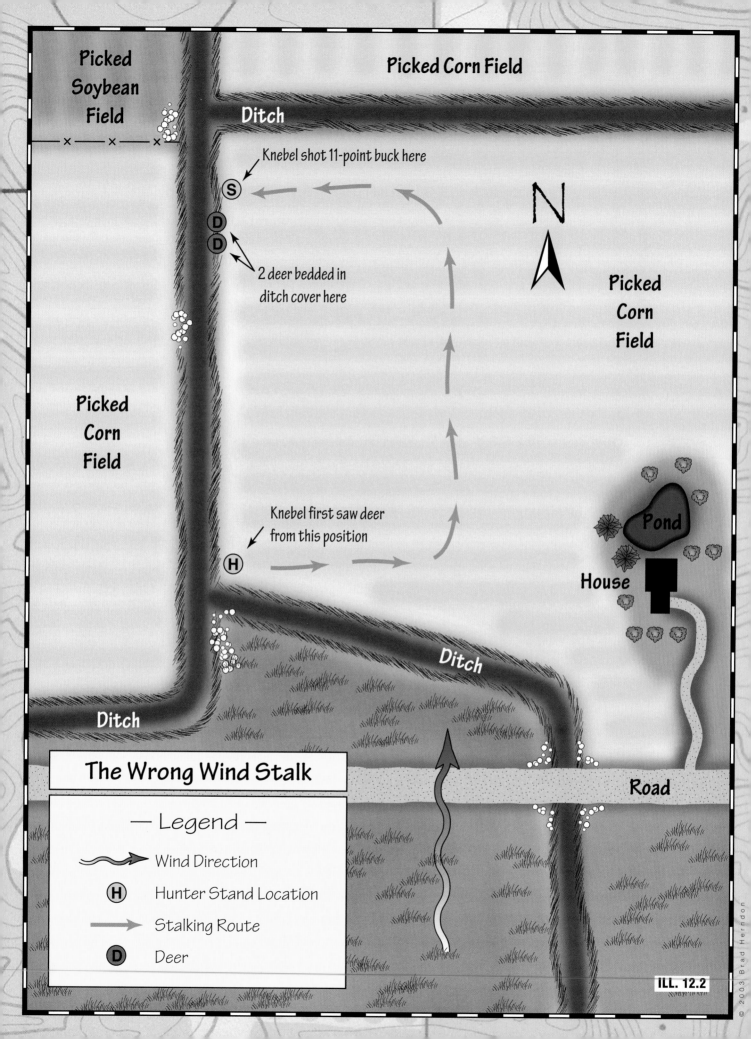

Picked Soybean Field

Picked Corn Field

Ditch

Knebel shot 11-point buck here

2 deer bedded in ditch cover here

Picked Corn Field

Picked Corn Field

Knebel first saw deer from this position

Pond

House

Ditch

Ditch

Road

The Wrong Wind Stalk

— Legend —

Wind Direction

H Hunter Stand Location

Stalking Route

D Deer

ILL. 12.2

© 2003 Brad Herndon

fencerows and a ditch both came into play in this stalk. Both of these can be easily found on a aerial map, by the way. The lone oak tree in the cut cornfield allowed Knebel to observe the deer and watch where they bedded. After the deer were bedded and settled down, Knebel noted their location carefully, then eased down the tree. Using the tree trunk and a sloping field for cover, he eased over into the deep ditch. This allowed him to move undetected toward the deer.

Along the way, Knebel would peek up every so often to note his position in relation to the deer's location. Once on the deer, he got the buck to stand up, making for a close 35 yard shot. Do take note here of the wind direction and how it was used. The whitetails didn't have a clue a hunter was anywhere near them.

The second map, **Illustration 12.2**, is extremely interesting because it shows the novel way in which Knebel took a seemingly bad wind and still ended up with a smile on his face. Actually Knebel was upwind from the whitetails when he saw thembed in the ditch cover but because he was over one half mile away, the wind dispersed his scent before it reached them.

By sneaking east one fourth of a mile, Knebel was able to get his scent out of the wind stream of the deer as he made his stalk. By creeping to the north up through the cut cornfield, he was able to get downwind of the bedded deer, then slip over to the ditch. Once there, he simply used the cover growing on the ditch bank to close

Although it seems unlikely, trophy whitetails live in fencerow country like this in south central Iowa. Figure out how to hunt fencerows and you may kill the buck of your dreams.

in for the kill. The buck, shot at 1:45 p.m., turned out to be an 11-pointer that grossed 145 $^6/_8$ inches.

Why Don't More Hunters Kill Fencerow Phantoms?

After reading about Steve Knebel's advice, and looking at his maps of successful hunts, the same question may come to your mind as came to mine: Why aren't more hunters successful in tagging these fencerow phantoms? Knebel can tell us why.

"I'm not the only person with permission to hunt these farms, " Knebel said. "Nor am I the only hunter to see these bucks. Most hunters, however, see a good buck and doe bed in a little thin fencerow and due to lack of confidence they don't even try a stalk. They just assume there is no possible way to get within shooting range of the buck, so they go on ahead. The truth is, there usually are several options available to you if you think about it long enough. Oftentimes, you can use two or even three different approaches to the deer. Naturally good luck doesn't hurt anything, and I have had my share of that, too."

What Knebel says is true, of course, but before ending

By using the terrain strategies revealed in this book, you'll find it's easy to fill your doe tags. Harvesting does helps to control the deer herd and they also provide delicious meat.

this chapter, it should be pointed out that a lot of this stalking is tough work. A heavy fencerow may mean the stalk can be made with an upright walk. No cover at all may necessitate a grindingly slow crawl. A high spot in a cornfield may afford you some terrain to cover your movements, but depending on the height of the rise, oftentimes it dictates an agonizingly painful stooped walk.

Still, all in all, the pain would be well worth the gain. Can you imagine the excitement of shaking a fence and watching a head full of horns jump up only 15 yards away? And can you imagine the feeling of accomplishment of standing over an awesome fencerow phantom, a whitetail among the most difficult of all to outwit?

As Always, Details Are Important

Throughout this book I have emphasized how important record keeping is to the success of many of the nation's top whitetail hunters. Steve Knebel is no different. He logs every hunt he makes, noting weather conditions, type of terrain, and type of hunting method used, such as stalking, still-hunting, or tree stand hunting. He

also lists the total number of deer seen, plus the rough score of any bucks he observed. Time spent on stand, still-hunting and stalking also is recorded.

By using a county plat book, Knebel can determine where property lines are located. These then can be transferred onto topographical and aerial maps, if desired. The topographical and aerial maps also let Knebel get a look at fencerows, ditches and other terrain features where he hunts. He uses aerial maps extensively because they show timber and brush features better than topo maps. A quick look at an aerial map when stalking a deer can oftentimes help him figure out an approach on a monster buck.

Typically Knebel stays in contact with around 70 landowners. This takes a lot of time and effort, but assures him of having a variety of locations in which to hunt. He doesn't own or lease any hunting land. Once more, this reveals the importance of having a good work ethic when it comes to chasing trophy deer. Knebel prefers to have person-to-person contact with landowners, even though they all know him. They keep him informed of deer they have seen on their property, sometimes reporting in late summer that they have "seen the trophy for this year" already. This hard work results in Knebel having nearly 11,000 acres on which to hunt. This land, however, is not exclusively his to hunt; other hunters use it as well.

Camo patterns Steve Knebel favors when hunting fencerows and ditches are Cornstalk camo and waterfowl camo such as Advantage Wetlands and Advantage MAX-4 (blaze orange is worn with the camo in firearms season). All of these patterns work great in most situations in which he hunts, matching well with foxtail grass and most other types of cover found in or around fencerows, or on ditch banks. These include weeds, cattails, small brush, willows, and picked soybean and corn stubble.

At first light, and late evening, Knebel spends time in a tree in order to locate a good buck in the open farm country where he hunts. Midday he still-hunts ditches, or glasses fencerows with a spotting scope or binoculars, looking for bedded trophies. Knebel has found whitetails aren't too particular about which fencerow they bed in as long as they can see a long distance. His personal experience is that fencerows at least ¼ mile away from the nearest timber are best.

Although I haven't mentioned weapons much in this book, a 12-gauge shotgun, equipped with a slug barrel with rifle sights, did the job for Steve Knebel on northern Indiana's brute bucks for many years. He recently switched to a scoped single-barrel shotgun. His shots are surprisingly close, averaging 25 or 30 yards, so a scope wouldn't be necessary in many of his hunting situations. On the few longer shots he takes, the scoped gun comes in handy. In states where high-powered rifles are legal and the plains stretch out for miles, certainly a scoped gun proves invaluable for long-range shots.

Maps Are Always Important

Regardless of where you hunt bucks, maps can be instrumental in your success. This is true whether you are a tree stand hunter, a still hunter, or a person who loves to stalk deer. Flat land is one instance where aerial maps are better than topographical maps, although both of them should be consulted when hunting.

When studying aerial maps, look for fencerows that connect tracts of timber, since deer will hold to these brushy fencerows as they move about during the day. Also be on the lookout for converging fencerows that come together at one location. There are more of these hubs out there than you might think, though many of them won't

Carry a map with you wherever you hunt. They are great for speed scouting a new region.

With today's great camo patterns, hunters can take Pope & Young bucks while hunting on the ground.

MY FAVORITE STAND

When bow hunting, a fencerow is probably my favorite stand site. During firearms season, I still love to hunt stands I've placed in fencerows. But my favorite stand location when using a firearm is any tree where I can place my tree stand very high and glass a large region of flat, generally open farm country.

On Thanksgiving morning in 2002 I was in a lone tree in an open field glassing hundreds of acres of farmland consisting of mostly ditches, fencerows and picked soybean and cornfields. In mid-morning I watched a shooter buck and a doe bed down near a fencerow that was south of me a few hundred yards. A smaller buck came into the same area later on in the morning, but I couldn't see where he bedded. The field north of me sloped off from the tree so I was able to sneak out of there and go eat Thanksgiving dinner with my family.

In the afternoon I came back and came in from the north on the opposite side of the fencerow from where the big buck was bedded with the doe. This approach was perfect for the southwest wind I had. The ground was very crunchy so I slipped along very slowly. Occasionally I uttered some soft grunts with my deer call. When I was closing in on the buck, I kept looking for the other buck because I knew he could ruin my hunt. Sure enough, when I was about 60 yards away from the shooter buck, the smaller buck jumped up and ran down the fencerow. When he did, I blew on my grunt call a few times. No other deer got up, so I figured I was still in business. In a few minutes I was in the exact location where the big buck should have been bedded with the doe. Hard as I tried, I couldn't see them.

Then, as they sometimes do, the big buck stood up on the other side of the fencerow, directly across from me. I raised the gun slowly and fired. When I did, broken weeds flew every which way and the buck toppled right over. What an exciting hunt! This is why I love hunting the way I do; you never know when you are going to come face to face with a monster. This deer was standing only 8 yards away when I made the fatal shot. He was a $4\frac{1}{2}$- year-old buck that grossed 148 inches.

So as odd as it seems, my favorite stand many times is in a tree that isn't even within shooting range of a deer trail.

Steve Knebel

---

be visible from any road. This is why you need to study the maps. Once you've located several hot fencerows or ditches, look at your topographical maps of the region to see if there are high spots in any fields which might serve as cover when you are moving about. Don't miss any detail on any map since it might be the missing clue instrumental to a successful hunt.

If you are a stand hunter you do have options even in vast stretches of flat land. In the absence of trees a ground blind of some type will often work. Native vegetation can be used in or near a fencerow or ditch to construct a blind. One can even be built in an open field if you do it well ahead of season and let the deer get used to its presence. The same goes for many excellent ground blinds now on the market. They conceal your movements, keep your scent dispersion down, and also help keep you warm on cold, brutal days. Again, these blinds must be put in position far enough ahead of time for the whitetails to get used to them. A few hunters even dig ground blinds in level areas with little cover. As I said, you do have several options when it comes to using a stand or ground blind in flat regions.

Tree Stands Aren't Everything

Almost all of this book entails the proper use of tree stands because they have been proven, by far, to be the most productive way of harvesting white-tailed deer, especially trophy deer. This chapter has been the exception. There are cases where still-hunting and stalking methods can be used, along with tree stand hunting, to harvest an older buck. Certainly still-hunting could be used in some way in hunting many of the strategic terrain locations I have described in other chapters.

For now, it's important for you to become an expert at using maps of all types in order to discover the terrain funnels deer will naturally move through. Once this is done, you can fine-tune your hunting to your particular style, as many have done before you. For most of you it may be tree stand hunting, as it is with me. For others it may be a combination of tree stand and still-hunting. And for still others it may be the most difficult hunting method of all—stalking. It has certainly worked for Steve Knebel, The Fencerow Master. Maybe it will for you.

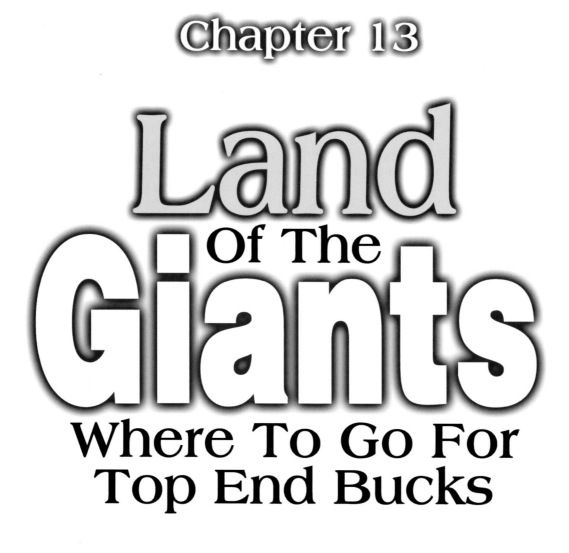

Chapter 13

Land Of The Giants

Where To Go For Top End Bucks

One evening in November of 1965, bow hunter Mel Johnson pulled his old 72-pound Howett recurve from his car and made his way to the edge of a soybean field. Crouching in a natural ground blind, Johnson wondered if he would see the big buck he had spotted earlier that fall. Less than an hour later Johnson had his answer. Excitedly he watched as a massive 12-point typical came venturing across the field toward him.

Amazingly, the trophy whitetail walked right to Johnson, getting so close to his blind he couldn't draw without being seen. Using great patience, he waited until the ancient buck was angling away from him and then zipped an arrow through the kill zone. The buck never made it out of the field. The deer ended up scoring 204-⁴/₈ inches, and has been the standing World Record archery typical ever since. The scene of this historic hunt was Peoria County, Illinois. As best I can tell, the details of this hunt indicate no strategic terrain funnel was involved in the demise of this World Record whitetail.

Since 1965 a few hunters have knelt beside deer and grabbed antlers that they thought would top Mel Johnson's magical mark, including eight bucks killed between 1993 and 2000 that have netted over 190 inches. None, however, even broke the 200-inch barrier. This almost changed because of a hunt Wayne Zaft made on October 8, 2001.

Zaft parked his truck that evening and made his way toward a line of brush that served as a travel corridor between two nice stands of timber. As he knelt down to check some deer tracks, he glanced up to see an absolutely monstrous buck coming toward him. When the giant deer trotted behind some thick cover, Zaft quickly moved closer to the bush line and stationed himself behind a broken off tree. An opening about 8 yards wide was in front of him about 34 yards away. It appeared the buck would come through this opening, so Zaft readied for the shot.

Mel Johnson's World Record archery typical was taken in 1965 in Peoria County, Illinois. It scores 204 4/8 inches and is representative of the great whitetails that come from The Prairie State. Photo courtesy of Legendary Whitetails

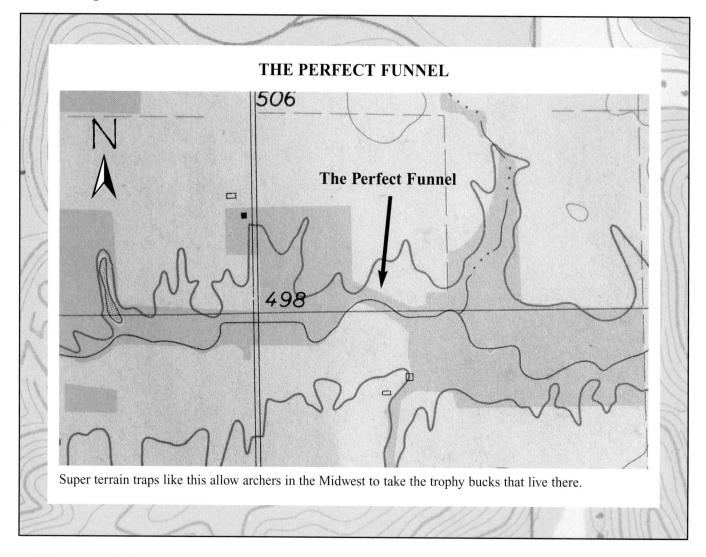

THE PERFECT FUNNEL

The Perfect Funnel

Super terrain traps like this allow archers in the Midwest to take the trophy bucks that live there.

When the tall-tined whitetail entered the shooting lane, Zaft grunted. The buck kept its pace. Another grunt from Zaft's mouth slowed the deer's pace, and knowing time was running out, Zaft squeezed the trigger on his release. Sickeningly, Zaft saw the arrow hit high and back. Unable to find the deer that evening, he spent a restless night and was back on the track first thing the next morning. Two fruitless hours were spent looking for the megabuck before he had to go to work. After a torturously long day at work, afternoon found Zaft searching once more. Still no sign of the deer.

Then, as so many world-class deer hunts do, the story takes a strange twist. It seems Zaft's adjacent landowner had discovered a huge buck lying dead in the middle of his field. It was Zaft's buck. Unfortunately, despite Zaft's dedicated efforts to recover the buck, coyotes had already gotten to the deer, destroying the carcass. Although this happens often in Canada because of the number of predators, it does not detract from the magnificence of deer's antlers.

While most hunters thought it would take another typical 12-point, or even a typical 14-point to break Mel Johnson's enduring record, this didn't seem to be the case. The Zaft buck carries a typical 11-point frame with 2 sticker points, making it a 13-point. However, since the right G5 tine doesn't have a matching tine on the left side, its 4 3/8 inch length is a total deduction. The rest of the rack makes up for this deduction.

Inside spread is 20 7/8 inches, main beams tally 28 6/8 and 27 7/8 inches and the deer carries an impressive 44 3/8 inches of mass. Seven of the tines go over 10 inches in length, with four of them stretching over 13 inches. The longest tine is 14 5/8 inches. Add everything up and the deer grosses 222 6/8 inches as a typical! After an asymmetry deduction of 11 7/8 inches and abnormal point deduction of 4 0/8 inches, the initial final net typical score was 206 7/8 inches! A new World's Record--if the Zaft buck's score held up when panel measured.

The Pope & Young Club's rulebook states the top 5 bucks must be scored by a panel of experienced measurers. This didn't occur until the spring of 2003, so when I wrote this book in 2002, I didn't know whether the Johnson or Zaft buck would hold the World's Record. Fortunately, I was able to make the final edit of this book in the summer of 2003 and could reveal the final results. The measuring panel decided the G3 (third) tine on the right main beam is non-typical because it comes from the G2 tine, not the main beam. This resulted in different tines being matched up, bringing the score down substantially. The Zaft buck ended up being one more great whitetail that fell short of Mel Johnson's legendary Illinois buck.

Still, it's a world-class looking buck all the way, and you may have noticed, as I did, that the Zaft buck was killed as it used a narrow travel corridor between two larger tracts of timber. My curiosity causes me to painstakingly read the stories of all top-end whitetails taken throughout North America, and I then try to deduct whether these great deer were taken from or near a strategic terrain funnel. Sometimes I can tell whether this is true or not, other times I can't. So while my curiosity doesn't allow me to accurately tell you what percent of book deer come from choke points such as I have detailed in this book, my curiosity does allow me to tell you what state, or other region of North America they come from.

This is true because many years ago I started recording into a database all whitetail entries, both typical and

The Boone & Crockett scoring system for whitetails is well respected and is used by the Pope & Young Club as well.

non-typical, from the Boone & Crockett and Pope & Young record books. To save time, at first I recorded only the state and score. When Carol took over my data entry chores ten years ago, she started entering the score, the state the book buck came from, and the county. On top-end deer she records the hunter's name as well. Because of her hard work, you are going to read some of the most detailed and accurate information ever accumulated regarding where book bucks come from.

This is what we're after.

Food plots for deer can be created to take advantage of terrain funnels located in the vicinity.

What The Archery Record Book Reveals

To make it easier to read, I've taken the United States and broken it up into regions. They are: Southeast, Northeast, Midwest, Northwest and Southwest. This should allow you to find your state rather quickly in the accompanying charts. I have also listed the Canadian provinces and Mexico.

For those of you whose favorite type of hunting is archery gear, you will quickly find the states that are tops for P & Y deer. Typical entries must score 125 inches or better to make the book, while non-typical entries must score 155 inches and up to qualify for the record book. And for those of you who might have your goal set at a higher scoring buck, I have listed the number of typical whitetail entries scoring 150 and higher, and also the number 170 inches or better. The same goes for the non-typical Pope & Young entries, with the scores listed for 170 inches and up, and 190 inches and up.

And don't overlook those entry figures for the last five years. I inserted these numbers so you can see which states have been cranking out quantities of mature whitetails in recent years. Take Wisconsin, for instance. Its typical entry numbers into the P & Y record book stand at the top of the heap with 4,771, yet entry numbers for the last five years total 2,025. This five-year figure represents over 42

percent of the all-time figure, so this shows Wisconsin is still hot as a firecracker for high-scoring deer. Buffalo County, specifically, is scorching hot, due to the prevalence of Quality Deer Management within the county.

To give you an idea of how Quality Deer Management (QDM) can impact the number of mature deer within a region, consider the following: In Buffalo County, Wisconsin typical bow kills qualifying for the P & Y record book have totaled an astonishing 273 entries over just the last 10 years! To put this in perspective, no all-time figures from any state in the southeast can top this figure. Only two states in the southwest can, four from the northwest, and five from the northeast. Of course the all-time entry numbers from the other eight states in the Midwest can beat Buffalo County's 273, but don't forget we're comparing one county to an entire state and a 10-year period to all-time figures. As I said, it's astonishing. Makes a guy want to lease or buy ground in Buffalo County, doesn't it?

The Top 10 Archery States

A list of the top 10 in any sport, activity or other category quickly draws the attention of a reader, whether the list is in a magazine, book, or on the Internet. These

Many states are implementing some form of Quality Deer Management. This will allow bucks such as this one to survive to maturity and turn into record-book whitetails.

top 10 articles are interesting for a variety of reasons, but what draws us to the list is that we want to see who, or what, is the best in the area, or the world. It's no different with deer hunting.

This is why I have included the top 10 typical and non-typical whitetail deer in both the Pope & Young and Boone & Crockett record books. They are the tops in the world in their respective categories and they give all of us a mark to shoot for. And to create even more interest among archers, I'm listing my picks for the top 10 states where the chances of harvesting a P & Y buck are the very highest. You will quickly notice, incidentally, how the number of entry figures from each state will not determine the rankings of my top 10 picks. Instead, I use a special formula to determine my list.

For example, it appears Wisconsin should lead the list because it has the most entries all-time and also for the past five years. Here's why it doesn't. Wisconsin's deer herd is over three times as large as the whitetail herd in Illinois. In a similar vein, the total number of bow hunters in Wisconsin is about three times greater than the

Some of the richest soils on earth are found in the Midwest and this contributes greatly to the growth rate of whitetails in the region.

number of archers in Illinois. In other words, in Wisconsin we have three times as many bow hunters hunting three times as many deer.

Despite this, Wisconsin's typical entries tally only 2,025 for the past five years compared to Illinois' 1,185. This number betters Illinois' entry figure by only 840 deer. It should be 2,370 since Wisconsin has three times as many bow hunters and deer. Simply put, for hours invested on stand, your opportunities at a book buck are going to be more frequent when bow hunting in Illinois than in Wisconsin.

Other factors I consider when determining my rankings are each state's management philosophy, the population trend of each state's whitetail herd, and even the effect of disease on the herd. The counties of Dane, Iowa and Sauk have recently contributed about 9 percent of Wisconsin's total entries. However, the discovery of chronic wasting

Practice all year to make sure you make the shot when a Pope & Young buck walks under your tree.

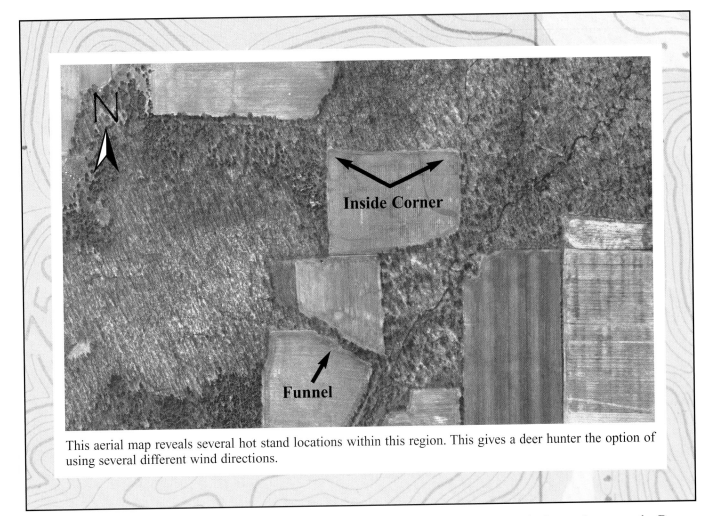

This aerial map reveals several hot stand locations within this region. This gives a deer hunter the option of using several different wind directions.

disease in the herd there has prompted a plan to eradicate all whitetails in parts of these three counties over the next five years. This involves an area of 361 square miles. Whether or not this plan moves ahead, it certainly is a factor I must consider. You will see in my list of top 10 counties that Dane and Sauk counties are the second and sixth best producers of book bucks in the state.

Examples of recent changes in state management strategies that will increase Pope & Young entry numbers are found in Indiana and Pennsylvania. The Hoosier State implemented a one antlered deer limit starting in 2002. Pennsylvania recently enacted a statewide antler point restriction that is expected to save 80,000 to 85,000 bucks the first year. As you can see, things change—and so do my predictions.

The Top Counties

For the first time ever, I have listed the top 10 counties for P & Y whitetails within the top 10 states. This information is as detailed as it can get. Not only do you now know the top states in which to hunt, you also know the best counties to head for. Let's look at a few of these top states for archery kills before going on to the Boone & Crockett statistics.

Illinois: Visions of vast stretches of flat fields containing corn and soybeans come to most deer hunter's minds when they think of Illinois. Containing some of the most fertile soil on earth, this state has the food, the genetics, and the management to grow huge deer. It has short, separated firearm seasons, with only the first three-day season falling within the rut. With only a few days to hunt, firearm hunters often fill their either sex license with an antlerless deer, most of them doe, allowing the bucks to grow to maturity. The P & Y figures reveal this is true.

Illinois has 798 typical Pope & Young entries scoring 150 inches or better, 88 scoring 170 inches and up. No other state comes close to these figures. To fully realize how staggering these statistics are, consider the following: If you take all the bucks scoring 150 inches or better from the southeast, northeast and northwest parts of our nation and add them all up, you would still have to add 235 more bucks to equal the number from Illinois!

Illinois produced the top typical whitetail with Mel Johnson's 204⁴/₈-inch giant from the distant past. Kent Anderson holds down the sixth spot with a 195²/₈-inch beast taken in 1999. Waiting to be officially measured is Ray Schremp's 196⅝-inch beauty taken in 2001. Illinois doesn't do too badly in the non-typical category, either, holding down the sixth and ninth positions. 2003 will bring the official measurement of an awesome deer Michael Ublish harvested in 2001. It will slip into the number 5 spot if its score of 254⅝ inches holds up.

As you often find in states with large cities, many of the top deer qualifying for Pope & Young from Illinois come from the suburbs. In fact, four of the top 10 counties in Illinois hug the city of Chicago, and another one is nearby. Other top 10 counties are found in the northwest, west central, central, and east central parts of the state. Obviously huge deer come from all over Illinois. There are no really bad places to hunt in Illinois, and this includes the southern part of the state where it's hilly.

I was once in the area photographing at the deer check stations during gun season. Carol and I were doing this because we wanted to see, first hand, just how many bruiser bucks were taken during this three-day hunt. At one check station we noticed a deer's rack sticking out of a trash bag at a little building where a taxidermist had set up shop. What he did was offer his taxidermy services to hunters as they checked in their deer. If the hunter was interested, the taxidermist caped the buck on the spot. I knew right away the trash bag buck was no ordinary deer. I measured it at 191⅝ inches net typical score!

In much of Illinois, you will find numerous flatland funnels exactly like the ones I have described in this book. An archer who hunts intelligently in Illinois should be able to slip his tag on more than one P & Y deer in his hunting career if he is selective.

Iowa, like Illinois, grows bucks of true top end quality, especially in the typical category. Seven of the top 20 typical whitetails in history have been tagged in The Hawkeye State! Four of these seven bucks have been taken in the last 10 years. The top 10 counties will be found in two general locations. On the east end of the state, the counties along or near the Mississippi river harbor a quantity of trophy whitetails. The other top-notch area is found in the south central part of the state, directly south and southeast of Des Moines.

As previously mentioned, Wisconsin's Buffalo County is a scorcher because of the amount of Quality Deer Management going on there. Four typical archery entries scoring over 170 have come from Buffalo County in the past two years, including Ken Shane's state record, a 189⅞-inch beauty. An easy way to find the hottest counties in Wisconsin is to place a point in

the middle of the state, and then draw one line southeast to Milwaukee, and another line directly west to the Mississippi River. Almost all counties falling within these two lines to the south are outstanding, although you do need to remember the chronic wasting disease eradication areas in the counties of Dane, Iowa and Sauk.

In Pursuit Of Monstrous Non-Typicals

Perhaps bow hunting's most intriguing story started back in the late 1950s along the Platte River, south of a Nebraska town named Shelton. Reports, it seems, began to surface of a huge buck that carried a bizarre looking rack. Catching wind of the story, Al Dawson of Hastings embarked on a memorable, but unsuccessful journey of pursuing bow hunting's greatest non-typical.

While hunting the Dan Thomas farm, one of his favorite locations, in 1958 Al saw this incredible whitetail coming his way, traveling with several does. The reports of the buck's strange antlers were true, with its weird drop tines along each side of its head giving it an unbalanced appearance. Out of desperation more than anything, Al released an arrow at the impressive animal, only to see the shaft fall short. Reliving the hunt in his mind later that day, Al thought the name "Mossy Horns" aptly described the unusual appearance of the deer's antlers and he vowed to kill this magnificent trophy whitetail.

Al hunted the rest of the 1958 season without sighting Mossy Horns again. In the fall of 1959, two other bow hunters, Gene Halloran and Charley Marlowe, joined in the chase for the elusive deer. Hunting from homemade platform tree stands, Al saw the deer twice that fall, the last time was on the final day of the season. Buoyed by this final glimpse of the monster deer, Al felt 1960 would be his year. And his thoughts almost became reality.

Unfortunately he shoulder shot Mossy Horns in 1960, resulting in the buck crashing and stumbling around near a fence. Strangely, no blood was found from the wound. The deer was not seen the rest of the season by any of the hunting group, who by now included a convert to the sport, a man named Del Austin. Even more disappointing, Dan never saw Mossy Horns on his farm during the next summer months, leading the hunters to believe perhaps the monarch had died, either from Al's arrow, or from old age, since the buck was believed to be 8 years old by then.

1961 brought nothing of the deer until near the end of the archery season, when on a cold, blustery day, Al Dawson felt a warm rush of blood wildly course through his veins. Coming his way were two antlered bucks, and one of them was Mossy Horns, alive and well! Although

Old Mossy Horns, Del Austin's World Record archery non-typical, has it all; beauty, character, a high score—2797/8 inches— and one of the most fascinating deer hunting stories in history. Photo courtesy of Legendary Whitetails

Using camo to match the terrain will assure that a monster buck won't pick you off when you make your draw on him.

High-scoring trophy bucks are still taken by archers using long bows. This tall-tined Indiana deer has a gross score of 166 inches despite the fact it has one major tine broken off.

interesting, one of the long drop tines had a one half-inch three blade cut in its length. Al had not shoulder shot Mossy Horns after all; he had staggered the great buck with a blow to its antlers! In four years of hunting Mossy Horns, no archer had been able to draw blood.

Hopes were high when the 1962 Nebraska archery season opened. Al, though, seemed to be destined to tag this great whitetail, for he saw Mossy Horns three times in early October, once again sending an errant arrow toward the multi-pointed whitetail. Then in late October, the five-year quest drew to an end.

Gene and Al arrived at the river bottom early and had taken stands, while Charley and Del left Hastings after work, arriving late. Del placed a portable platform stand in an island of dense brush. Standing on his platform shortly before dark, Del glanced over when a loud racket from upwind drew his attention. It was Mossy Horns, and he was coming directly toward Del!

When the great buck stopped broadside at 20 yards, the wise old whitetail steered clear of Al's tree stand, the deer looked, from all appearances, to be a World Record non-typical.

Dan Thomas documented this in the spring of 1962 with the discovery of a set of shed antlers from old Mossy Horns. Giving the deer an estimated inside spread, the final score tallied an amazing 281 inches! And almost as Del drew back his 45-pound Oneida recurve and placed an arrow tipped with a Bear Razorhead in Mossy Horns' kill zone. What may be the most fascinating hunt in history for a trophy whitetail was finally over. The efforts all the hunters exerted, especially Al Dawson, certainly were worth the wait. With double drop tines near the bases, Mossy Horns has an astonishing total of 95^{2}/$_{8}$

Larry Raveling's Rag Horn buck is the number five deer in the non-typical category of the Boone & Crockett record book. Raveling missed this 282-inch monster in 1972 when it had a pair of white drawers impaled on its antlers. The next year he had a rare second chance at the buck and made good on the shot. Photo courtesy of Legendary Whitetails

inches of abnormal points. Add in the 184$\frac{5}{8}$ inch net typical score and you come up with an archery non-typical World Record of 279$\frac{7}{8}$ inches, a score that has now stood the test of time for almost 40 years.

Many hunters feel this record may never be broken. But if it is broken, it could very well come from the state of Kansas.

Kansas' reputation for gnarly old non-typicals is well deserved since Kansas bow hunters have killed 6 out of the top 10 non-typicals in history. The biggest is a 262$\frac{7}{8}$ inch trophy Dale Larson tagged in 1998. Of the 14 archery non-typicals in history scoring over 240 inches, 7 of them have been taken in Kansas. There are super typicals in Kansas as well. Brad Henry did his share in 2001 to make Kansas bow hunters proud when he took a giant 193$\frac{7}{8}$-inch typical. This is the top P & Y typical from Kansas and presently ranks number 10 all-time. Kansas has 16 P & Y entries netting over 180 inches. 8 of them have been tagged within the past 10 years.

Whether hunting for a gigantic typical or non-typical in Kansas, the entire region east of Salina and Wichita, about one third of the state, offers you the highest odds of success. Best counties for both typical and non-typical deer are Butler, Washington, Pottawatomie, Greenwood, Linn and Sedgwick.

By taking an atlas, such as the one from Rand McNally, and going to the index in the back, you can quickly find the locations of all other counties I have listed in the accompanying charts. All of the states offer excellent hunting and with a little work you will uncover the hottest geographic regions within each.

Boone & Crockett Bucks

On November 20, 1914 near Danbury, Wisconsin James Jordan and his friend Egus Davis ventured out on a hunt for whitetails. Egus was the first one to taste success, tagging a doe that would provide his family with winter meat. After helping Egus field-dress the doe, James continued to still-hunt in the snow, soon coming upon the tracks of a large deer who was traveling in the company of several other deer. As James paused to listen to the lonesome whistle of a train on a nearby track, a group of deer jumped up in front of him. One was a huge buck and James emptied his .25/20 Winchester at it as it fled the scene.

After tracking the whitetail for some distance, James caught up with the deer as it crossed a river. He used his last shell to finish off the magnificent animal. When James saw the buck, he immediately realized it was the biggest whitetail he had ever seen. With a live body weight estimated at 400 pounds, and antlers containing 10-points with incredible mass, this was one special deer. So even though whitetails weren't as popular back then as they are now, and quality taxidermy still was in the infancy stage, James still decided to have the massive deer mounted.

As fate would have it, a man named George VanCastle came to admire the deer, and since he was a part-time taxidermist, James elected to have him do the mounting job. The cost was $5. James watched as George carried his incredible buck onto the Soo Train line for his trip back to nearby Webster. James expected to see the deer mounted in a few months. Instead, because of ill health in George's family requiring them to move, it was several decades before James again saw the antlers of what was, unbeknown to him, the greatest typical whitetail ever to have been taken by a hunter in modern history!

Continuing this saga, In 1964 Bob Ludwig, an employee of the Minnesota DNR, was at a rummage sale in Sandstone, Minnesota when he noticed a massive set of antlers with a $3 price tag on them. He thought the rack worthy of the price and purchased it. Shortly thereafter Bob read an article about scoring whitetails according to the Boone & Crockett system. Using this method, Bob came up with an astonishing score of 205 inches—a new World Record!

Then in a twist of fate which goes totally beyond belief, Bob Ludwig one day invited a long-lost cousin who he had not seen in some time in to see the mounted deer. A strange look creased the wrinkled face of the old man as he admired the great whitetail. The man was James Jordan, and he was looking at his buck for the first time in 50 years!

As time evolved, Bob had the rack officially scored and in 1971 a panel of B & C measurers made this mysterious 10-point buck the new official World Record typical at 206$\frac{1}{8}$ points. Ironically, no one knew who killed the buck, when it was killed, or even what state was responsible for growing a whitetail of such proportions, for no one was yet convinced James Jordan had indeed been the successful hunter.

This was true because no eyewitnesses were still alive who had seen the deer back in 1914. Finally, though, through a combined effort of many individuals over a period of years, enough evidence was gathered to convince all concerned parties that James Jordan truly was the man who killed the typical world-record whitetail. Sadly, this announcement became official in December of 1978 — two months after James Jordan died at the age of 86!

To this day, the words "The Jordan Buck" have a ring to them which is more familiar to whitetail enthusiasts nation-wide than any other deer in history. Although this

It's an accomplishment to get your name in one of the record books. Sound hunting strategies will help you accomplish this feat.

is partly true because of the deer and the hunter's storied past, the rack itself has a magical, captivating quality too.

For a 10-point frame to score 206⅛ inches, it has to have everything; spread, height, main beam length, symmetry and mass. The Jordan buck has all of these, plus beauty. The main beams are both 30 inches long, spread is 20⅛ inches, and two tines stretch to over 13 inches long. Mass is impressive, with the eight circumference measurements totaling a staggering 54⅝ inches!

Yes, the history behind The Jordan Buck is fascinating. It seems, though, that there is always something mysterious, intriguing, or unlikely involved in every successful hunt that has produced a world-class deer. Take the Milo Hanson buck, the new typical World Record from Biggar, Saskatchewan, Canada, for an example. This awesome 213⅝ inch, 14-pointer (a basic 6 x 6 with

two sticker points) was taken November 23, 1993 by Milo Hanson while he and some of his friends were "pushing the bush."

Unlike the Jordan buck that took decades to be recognized as a World Record, the world knew about the Hanson buck within a couple of days. This success story could just as easily have been a tale of woe. When Milo fired several rounds at the buck, one of them struck the deer's right main beam between the G1 and G2 tines, weakening it considerably, but not breaking it off. Milo Hanson's deer came within a quarter of an inch of being a one antlered buck instead of a World Record! Such is the stuff monster buck stories are made of.

Qualifying Scores For Boone & Crockett

A whitetail must net 170 inches or better to qualify for the all-time typical category, while the minimum entry score for an all-time non-typical deer is 195 inches. B & C does have a three-year awards program where the entry scores are lower, 160 inches for a typical, 185 for a non-typical.

The Boone & Crockett record book is not simply big game record book for gun kills. Bow kills may be entered in the Boone & Crockett record book as well. Bow kills hold top positions in several states in the B & C record book. Mel Johnson's 204 4/8 inch Illinois typical and Del Austin's 277 3/8 inch non-typical from Nebraska are two that come to mind. The P & Y scoring system came from, and is the same as, the B & C scoring system. Due to different measurers, however, the same buck may have slightly differing scores in the two record bucks. Such is true with the Del Austin buck.

Also, you will see some great bow kills in the Boone & Crockett record book that aren't in Pope & Young. This occurs because P & Y entry rules state a compound bow may not have a greater letoff than 65 percent. Many modern compound bows surpass this figure, so deer taken while the hunter is using such a bow don't qualify for P & Y, but do qualify for the B & C book.

One other difference is found in the Boone & Crockett and Pope & Young record books. Boone & Crockett accepts dead deer — pickups — that have been found by people, while Pope & Young doesn't. And some of these deer are very interesting.

Consider the deer holding the top two positions in Boone & Crockett's non-typical whitetail category.

In 1981 a monstrous non-typical buck was found dead beside a fence in St. Louis County, Missouri. Carrying 44 points, this deer scored 333 7/8 inches. It shattered the long-standing World Record! Think about it. This is close to 50 inches — more than four feet — more than the Texas buck scored. The whitetail world was stunned. Surely the zenith of non-typical scores had been realized in the discovery of this great deer.

However, as strange as it may seem, a whitetail of similar proportions had been hanging in a bar in Kent, Ohio since the early 1940s. Like the St. Louis County buck, this deer had not been taken by a hunter, but was found dead along a railroad track. Dubbed the Hole-In-The-Horn buck because of a hole about the size of a .22 caliber bullet in one of its drop tines, this deer was discovered by Dick Idol in 1983. Scored unofficially by two measurers at over 342 inches, this 45-point brute looked like a sure bet to take the non-typical score up still one more level. It was not to be.

When scored by the Boone & Crockett panel in 1986, they deemed the Hole-In-The-Horn buck carried a basic 8-point typical frame, not a 10-point typical frame. Because of this judgment call, the massive rack scored "only" 328 2/8 inches, thus making it second on the all-

time list. Many hunters still believe this deer have the largest rack in history. From the looks of it I cannot disagree, even though it currently holds the number two position in the record book. Certainly its story is among the most intriguing in whitetail history. Only recently has a man came forward with details on the discovery of the Hole-In-The-Horn buck. He put to rest the mystery of how the hole was placed in the drop tine.

According to George Winters, the deer was, in truth, killed by a train near the Ravenna arsenal in Ohio in the early 1940s. Evidently after being hit by the train, the buck struggled down the railroad embankment to a fence that bordered the arsenal. Once there, its rack became entangled in the fence, with one of the rigid wires from the fence piercing the porous drop tine. George, who was patching potholes at the arsenal, actually helped free the rack from the fence so it would not be damaged, thereby preserving intact one of nature's greatest trophies.

A few hunters hold the opinion these huge, multi-pointed deer are sterile and therefore don't participate in the rut. Since this means they don't move in search of does, they would be much harder for a hunter to kill. Fascinatingly, over the past 10 years my records show 40 non-typical deer netting over 200 inches have been pickups, or about 1 in every 38 entries.

There Are Differences In Statistics

As we look at the Boone & Crockett record book versus the Pope & Young record book, it doesn't take long to see there are substantial differences, ratio-wise, in the entries for some regions. There are, for the most part, reasons for these varying numbers.

Let's look at Canada first. Bow entries from Canada are, overall, small in number. Firearm entries into the B & C record book, meanwhile, are extremely high. There are 191 typical archery entries from Alberta and 81 from Saskatchewan. Twenty –two states rank ahead of Alberta in the archery record book. Thirty rank ahead of Saskatchewan. Turning to the Boone & Crockett record book we'll find Alberta with 186 typical entries, Saskatchewan with 290. Only seven states have more B & C entries than Alberta. Even fewer states; four, have more typical entries than Saskatchewan. Here are the reasons for those huge disparities between the two record books.

First of all, there are few bow hunters in Canada. Deer herds are small as well. Take into consideration, too, that the temperature may be well below zero, accompanied by howling winds, when the rut is going full force. These conditions are not favorable for the bow hunter. This means most deer hunters push the bush

With a score of 2014/8 inches, the Wayne Bills' buck ranks number eight all-time in the Boone & Crockett typical category. Taken in 1974 in Hamilton County, Iowa, it is considered one of the most beautiful deer ever killed by a hunter. Photo courtesy of Legendary Whitetails

with a rifle in their hand, or if they aren't using this method of hunting, they are sitting in a cozy little wooden blind where they are protected from the brutal elements of the frozen north.

These reasons, and the fact hunters from the states are going to have $3,000 or more dollars invested in an archery hunt in Canada, is why I didn't pick Alberta or Saskatchewan as one of my top bow picks. If you love to rifle hunt, and you have deep pockets, without question Alberta and Saskatchewan are two great places to hunt trophy whitetails. The next deer past your stand could be a World Record. There have been 14 bucks topping 190 inches taken from Saskatchewan alone, and 58 over 180 inches. Alberta's best whitetail is Stephen Jansen's 204 2/8-inch monster. Alberta has produced six bucks over 190, 40 over 180 inches. In total, 701 trophies scoring 180 or higher have been entered in the Boone & Crockett record book. Alberta and Saskatchewan account for 98, or 14 percent of this total.

Another territory I want to discuss is Maine. Similar to Canada, Maine has an extremely low number of Pope & Young entries, while the Boone & Crockett numbers are pretty decent.

"Maine is big woods hunting," noted my good friend Bill Vaznis. "There are bogs, hills, mountains, and some agriculture. There aren't many deer, though. If you want to succeed in Maine, you need to be a woodsman. You need to be more than a great shot. You need to have a map in one hand and a compass in the other. If you really know how to hunt, you can kill some great deer there."

Many of the same factors working against bowhunters in Canada, can also be found in Maine. Finding strategic deer funnels in Maine could put you on some great deer no one else is hunting in both bow and firearms seasons.

Going to the southeastern part of the United States, Georgia is a state that is quite puzzling to me. Look at the all-time archery numbers — 184 typical, 9 non-typical. The top typical bow kill is only 159 1/8 inches, leading one to believe Georgia doesn't grow big whitetails. The Boone & Crockett record book proves otherwise. The top firearm typical scores an outstanding 191 4/8 inches and a total of 113 typical and 30 non-typical deer have made the B&C book. The top non-typical, by the way, goes 240 3/8 inches, again a great whitetail.

Of course all 113 typical Boone & Crockett entries top the state-record typical archery buck, proving there are many whitetails roaming around in Georgia that would topple the current archery state-record. If an archer wants to break a current state record, in my opinion there is no better state in which to do it than Georgia. The west central and southwest parts of the state are the best producers.

For the firearm hunter in the southeast part of our nation, Georgia is my top pick for Boone & Crockett bucks. Quality Deer Management, both on an individual and state level, is growing, so the future looks bright. My second pick in the southeast is Arkansas. As the figures show, the southeast doesn't have the deer genetics and other conditions to grow as many high-scoring trophies as the states in the Midwest. This is not to say you should get complacent while deer hunting in the southeast. A real heart-stopping buck mysteriously shows up there every so often.

Ask James McMurray of Louisiana; it happened to him. It occurred on January 4, 1994 when McMurray made a hunt on public land.

It was a cold day for Louisiana. McMurray watched for a few minutes as the black sky spit out first snow, then sleet. A 10 mph wind cut against his insulated coveralls. Presently McMurray made a rattling sequence, accompanied with several grunts. As he waited for 15 minutes he felt confident. During his walk in he had seen plenty of fresh deer tracks. Again he rattled and grunted, and waited another 15 minutes. The third time McMurray sent the sounds of a buck fight out into the dense thicket, a deer responded.

At first, he could see only a patch of brown coming his way. Then the top of antler tines became visible. Yes, a buck was coming in, intent on looking for the combatants in his region. Picking out a 2-foot square opening, McMurray put the crosshairs of his scope on the buck's shoulder and, as the deer passed through the opening, he touched off the shot.

As McMurray watched the buck disappear in the brush, he knew he had made a fatal hit. He couldn't have known, however, that he had just downed one of the highest scoring non-typical whitetails in history. At this time, the 29-point giant with a net score of 281 6/8 inches ranks as the sixth highest scoring whitetail ever recorded in the Boone & Crockett non-typical category.

The Anthony Fulton buck from Mississippi is another beast that showed up in an unlikely place, the southeast. Taken in 1995, this whitetail was one of the most difficult in history to accurately measure due to the configuration of the rack. After much consideration, this whitetail finally entered the Boone & Crockett record book at 295 6/8 inches, making it the third highest scoring non-typical whitetail in history, and the highest scoring non-typical ever taken by a hunter. As I said, although the southeast isn't the top trophy area of our nation, don't fall asleep on stand. The buck of many lifetimes might walk by while you're snoozing.

This 9-point Midwest bruiser missed making the Boone & Crockett typical entry score of 170 by just 2 inches.

Count the points. It's a 7 x 7 typical. You don't see many whitetail bucks with this type of typical frame. This deer has 26-points and its typical frame grosses 223⁵/₈ inches. Due to numerous deductions, it nets "only" 190²/₈ inches as a typical.

Other Boone & Crockett Picks

In the northeast, Maine and Maryland are the two states growing the most B & C bucks. At this time they are my top picks for book bucks in this region. As Quality Deer Management continues to expand in states like New York, Virginia and Pennsylvania, look for the quantity of mature whitetails to increase substantially in these states. Maine consists of vast tracts of timber and presents a perfect opportunity to those enjoying the beauty of nature in a deep-woods setting. If hunting in a more compact situation in a rural setting is more to your liking and fits your present hunting skills, then Maryland is a fine place to be. High-scoring bucks come from both states. The top 10 bucks in Maine all net over 180 inches. The top eight bucks from Maryland also net over 180.

Moving on to the Midwest, we come to the heart of big whitetail country, and to a wealth of fabled deer hunting stories. I've already shared information about the James Jordan buck from Wisconsin, the legendary Hole-In-The-Horn non-typical from Ohio, and the World Record non-typical from St. Louis County, Missouri.

These stories are only a fraction of the compelling, and true, stories to be read about Midwest whitetail hunting.

One year just before Christmas I received a letter from a man named Larry Lawson of Anderson, Indiana. I read with fascination as he inquired if I would be interested in doing a story about a deer he had just recently killed. Out of curiosity I called him — and ended up doing a story about a new World Record whitetail. In this case it was a World Record typical for the muzzleloader division of The Longhunter's Society.

You'll see walls of mounted deer if you attend the Illinois Deer Classic or other similar shows around the country.

The buck netted 187$^{1}/_{8}$ inches.

A couple of years after this, a guy pulled into my driveway one afternoon wanting me to measure a big 10-pointer he had taken that morning. I had just gotten in from deer hunting, and although I was tired I agreed to score the buck. It proved to be a surprise for me because the whitetail's rack had two tall curving brow tines. It was a buck I had been hunting for two years!

I was just finishing up the measuring session when another young man pulled into my driveway. He was driving an older pickup truck with the tailgate closed and wanted to know if he could look at the other guy's deer. "Sure," I said, "It's a great buck. It nets 162 even."

For some reason, as the young man looked at the 10-point buck, I walked around behind his truck and happened to glance in the bed. I almost fainted! One of the most awesome non-typicals I had ever seen was in the back. In a flash, everyone in my driveway was gathered around this new find. The young man's name was Larry Deaton and he had taken this great trophy while he was

hunting with a handgun. His whitetail ended up with a score of 229$^{7}/_{8}$ inches, and became the new non-typical World Record handgun kill.

Stories like this abound in the Midwest simply because the fertile terrain is ideal for growing outstanding bucks. This is why if you look at my top 10 Boone & Crockett picks, eight out of the nine Midwestern states make the list. The only states from other parts of the nation to crack the top 10 are Kansas and Texas.

As you look at the top 10 chart, some of you may be surprised to see Kentucky listed so high at number four. I can understand why. Kentucky is a "sleeper" state. If panel judging approves its score, Kentucky will have a typical in the B & C book scoring 204$^{2}/_{8}$ inches. Yet the Bluegrass State gets little press. As the old saying goes, figures don't lie, so when I crunched the numbers for the past five years of Boone & Crockett entries, Kentucky came out at number four. Only the whitetail entries for the past five years from Illinois, Iowa and Wisconsin can top Kentucky. With a one antlered deer per year limit and great deer management throughout the state, I expect the number of high scoring deer from this low-key state to remain good for the foreseeable future.

Buffalo County, Wisconsin is the top county in the nation when it comes to whitetails that make the record books.

You Have Choices In The Midwest

Several of the states in the Midwest, such as Indiana, Ohio, Illinois, and Iowa, allow a deer hunter to use only a shotgun, handgun or muzzleloading rifle. Other states like Kentucky, Missouri, Wisconsin and Michigan allow the use of high-powered rifles in selected areas. If you are traveling from another state to the Midwest for a deer-hunting trip, you should be able to find a state suitable for your type of hunting.

You can pick your weather conditions, too. If you don't mind bitter cold, northern Minnesota, Wisconsin or Michigan might be your choice. If you get cold easily while on stand, the temperatures are quite moderate in Kentucky, and in the southern parts of Missouri, Illinois, Indiana, and Ohio. If you just love to hunt whitetails, the Midwest is a great place to be afield. The region, without question, can offer you an opportunity to harvest the deer of your choice. Now, partner, let's mosey on over to the west.

Best Of The West

Texas, Kansas, Nebraska, and Montana are the best of the West. Next come South Dakota and Oklahoma. I've already covered Kansas in my Pope & Young picks, so I won't linger on it long. The eastern third of the state was the highest producer of archery book bucks, and it's also great for the firearm hunter. Regardless of that, don't overlook the more open western regions of Kansas. The trophies using this vast terrain are more vulnerable to a rifle hunter and some real dandies come from this section of the state. In places, land access in Kansas is still available for both the bow and firearm hunter, just for the asking.

Texas, as many of you know, consists of an incredible number of acres of managed deer habitat. To hunt big bucks there, you either have to own or lease land, or pay to hunt on ranches. Scrub brush, cactus, and other dry ground habitat may not look too appealing to some whitetail enthusiasts, but the big deer are tucked in there. A $284\frac{3}{8}$-inch non-typical buck, taken in Texas in1892, held the World Record for decades. Over the past five years, Texas hunters have tagged 45 typical and 19 non-typical Boone & Crockett bucks. The southern part of the state is the biggest producer.

In many of the Western states, you should be aware that many of the best scoring deer come from river bottom valleys. This is especially true of sections of Wyoming, Montana, Colorado, and several other states.

The statistics reveal a substantial number of entries from river systems from many sections of the United States. The record book entry numbers from counties along the Mississippi, Missouri, Ohio, and lesser rivers like the Des Moines River, account for a huge number of both Pope & Young and Boone & Crockett bucks. This holds true from north to south, with good P & Y entry numbers even coming from the counties bordering the Mississippi river where it divides Mississippi and Louisiana.

This chapter contains many statistics that will reveal, with a little study, the hottest trophy hunting regions of North America. If you master the terrain tactics detailed in this book, and then put your expert hunting skills to use in the best whitetail areas available to you, the results will most likely be successful beyond your imagination.

Top 10 State Picks For A Pope & Young Buck
1. Illinois
2. Iowa
3. Kansas
4. Wisconsin
5. Ohio
6. Indiana
7. Minnesota
8. Missouri
9. Nebraska
10. Kentucky

TOP 10 POPE & YOUNG COUNTIES

State: Illinois	State: Kansas	State: Ohio	State: Minnesota	State: Nebraska
1. Pike	1. Butler	1. Meigs	1. Morrison	1. Gage
2. Lake	2. Pottawatomie	2. Ross	2. Washington	2. Sarpy
3. McHenry	3. Shawnee	3. Vinton	3. Anoka	3. Lancaster
4. Lasalle	4. Bourbon	4. Licking	4. Dakota	4. Douglas
5. Brown	5. Washington	5. Athens	5. Winona	5. Cass
6. Peoria	6. Douglas	6. Delaware	6. Houston	6. Dakota
7. Jo Daviess	7. Sumner	7. Lawrence	7. Olmsted	7. Lincoln
8. Kane	8. Greenwood	8. Preble	8. Goodhue	8. Nemaha
9. Will	9. Linn	9. Gallia	9. Fillmore	9. Pawnee
10. Clark	10. Marion	10. Geauga	10. Hennepin	10. Clay

State: Iowa	State: Wisconsin	State: Indiana	State: Missouri	State: Kentucky
1. Allamakee	1. Buffalo	1. Parke	1. Boone	1. Hardin
2. Dubuque	2. Dane	2. Vigo	2. St. Louis	2. Todd
3. Van Buren	3. Columbia	3. Jefferson	3. Jackson	3. Christian
4. Warren	4. Trempealeau	4. LaPorte	4. Putnam	4. Shelby
5. Winneshiek	5. Waukesha	5. Marshall	5. Macon	5. Ohio
6. Appanoose	6. Sauk	6. St. Joseph	6. Pike	6. Union
7. Linn	7. Waupaca	7. Ripley	7. St. Charles	7. Harrison
8. Marion	8. Marquette	8. Greene	8. Callaway	8. Breckinridge
9. Des Moines	9. Rock	9. Kosciusko	9. Scotland	9. Jefferson
10. Monroe	10. Jefferson & Walworth (tie)	10. Martin	10. Clay & Adair (tie)	10. Crittenden

Indiana is one of the top 10 states for Pope & Young bucks. Tony Ray took this beautiful 196-inch non-typical from the southern part of the Hoosier state.

If you want to slip your deer tag on a Pope & Young buck in Missouri, Boone County is your best bet.

Rank	Score	Year	State	Hunter
1	204^4/$_8$	1965	Illinois	Mel Johnson
2	197^6/$_8$	1962	Iowa	Lloyd Goad
3	197^6/$_8$	1986	Minnesota	Curt Van Lith
4	197^1/$_8$	1991	Alberta	Don McGarvey
5	195^7/$_8$	1995	Minnesota	Barry Peterson
6	195^2/$_8$	1999	Illinois	Kent Anderson
7	194^2/$_8$	1977	Iowa	Robert L. Miller
8	194^0/$_8$	1981	Colorado	Stuart Clodfelder
9	194^0/$_8$	1994	Iowa	Steve Tyer
10	193^7/$_8$	2001	Kansas	Brad Henry

Pope & Young's Top 10 Typicals

The top 5 bucks in the Pope & Young record book must be panel measured. As noted in the text, the Zaft buck fell short of breaking the world's record. Another potential top 5 buck, taken by Ray Schremp in Illinois in 2000, was initially scored at 196 6/8 inches. It ended up scoring 193 6/8 inches, just missing the top 10 list.

Rank	Score	Year	State	Hunter
1	279^7/$_8$	1962	Nebraska	Del Austin
2	269^7/$_8$	2000	Missouri	Randy Simonitch
3	262^7/$_8$	1998	Kansas	Dale Larson
4	257^0/$_8$	1988	Kansas	Kenneth B. Fowler
5	250^6/$_8$	1994	Kansas	Kenneth R. Cartwright
6	250^4/$_8$	2000	Illinois	Andrew French III
7	249^6/$_8$	1968	Kansas	Clifford Pickell
8	246^3/$_8$	1992	Kansas	Richard Stahl
9	245^5/$_8$	1981	Illinois	Robert E. Chestnut
10	245^4/$_8$	1988	Kansas	Douglas A. Siebert

Pope & Young's Top 10 Non-Typicals

As noted above, the top 5 bucks must be panel measured by Pope & Young. Michael Ublish harvested a giant non-typical in Illinois on November 8, 2001 that scored 254 6/8 inches. Since it was a potential top 5 deer, it was also panel measured and came up with a score of 241 3/8 inches, making it another giant Illinois buck that just missed making a top 10 list of Pope & Young.

Southeast Pope & Young Typical Entries

	All-Time Entries	Last 5 Years Entries	Score 150 Up	Score 170 Up	Best Buck
Alabama	106	34	3	1	170^2/$_8$
Arkansas	170	55	14	1	170^0/$_8$
Florida	8	2	1	0	153^4/$_8$
Georgia	184	77	9	0	159^1/$_8$
Louisiana	81	35	8	2	175^2/$_8$
Mississippi	197	92	16	0	164^7/$_8$
North Carolina	91	33	5	0	161^0/$_8$
South Carolina	21	5	2	1	170^5/$_8$
Tennessee	104	30	9	1	172^6/$_8$

Northeast Pope & Young Typical Entries

	All-Time Entries	Last 5 Years Entries	Score 150 Up	Score 170 Up	Best Buck
Connecticut	112	40	10	0	$162^2/_8$
Delaware	34	14	4	1	$181^6/_8$
Maine	27	9	5	1	$174^4/_8$
Maryland	509	176	70	9	$183^3/_8$
Massachusetts	113	44	6	0	$157^5/_8$
New Hampshire	58	29	6	0	$157^3/_8$
New Jersey	278	95	16	1	$189^4/_8$
New York	681	309	58	4	$180^3/_8$
Pennsylvania	524	229	42	4	$175^6/_8$
Rhode Island	11	8	2	0	$160^4/_8$
Vermont	3	0	0	0	$140^7/_8$
Virginia	259	91	28	1	$182^6/_8$
West Virginia	288	135	41	2	$171^3/_8$

Midwest Pope & Young Typical Entries

	All-Time Entries	Last 5 Years Entries	Score 150 Up	Score 170 Up	Best Buck
Illinois	3497	1185	798	88	$204^4/_8$
Indiana	840	275	150	11	$190^4/_8$
Iowa	2038	753	506	74	$197^6/_8$
Kentucky	490	162	90	9	$188^2/_8$
Michigan	914	305	101	6	$193^2/_8$
Minnesota	1483	339	284	33	$197^6/_8$
Missouri	871	306	128	13	$179^0/_8$
Ohio	1543	522	293	27	$188^0/_8$
Wisconsin	4771	2025	560	38	$189^7/_8$

Southwest Pope & Young Typical Entries

	All-Time Entries	Last 5 Years Entries	Score 150 Up	Score 170 Up	Best Buck
Arizona	0	0	0	0	0
California	0	0	0	0	0
Colorado	127	38	31	4	$194^0/_8$
Kansas	1224	336	372	66	$193^7/_8$
Nevada	0	0	0	0	0
New Mexico	0	0	0	0	0
Texas	804	327	51	6	$173^7/_8$
Utah	0	0	0	0	0

Northwest Pope & Young Typical Entries

	All-Time Entries	Last 5 Years Entries	Score 150 Up	Score 170 Up	Best Buck
Idaho	47	13	7	0	$168^1/_8$
Montana	291	81	28	5	$176^4/_8$
Nebraska	468	180	77	6	$189^1/_8$
North Dakota	274	82	31	4	$173^3/_8$
Oregon	7	1	1	0	$153^7/_8$
South Dakota	349	82	46	3	$179^3/_8$
Washington	65	22	16	1	$175^1/_8$
Wyoming	56	20	2	0	$153^6/_8$

If you use the wind correctly while hunting choke points in states known for growing big deer, you should, at some point, find yourself at full draw on a trophy buck.

Corn, soybeans, alfalfa, clover, browse, fertile soil, and genetics—the Midwest has it all. That's why the record book entries from this region are unsurpassed.

Note! 25 of the state record typical Pope & Young bucks were taken within the past 10 years, 6 within the past 2 years.

Canada Pope & Young Typical Entries				
All-Time Entries	**Last 5 Years Entries**	**Score 150 Up**	**Score 170 Up**	**Best Buck**
Alberta	191	60	44	4	206⅞ (unofficial)
British Columbia	15	4	1	0	153⁶/₈
Manitoba	62	22	18	3	181⁴/₈
New Brunswick	9	2	1	0	166⁴/₈
Nova Scotia	3	1	0	0	137⁶/₈
Ontario	94	17	16	1	170⁰/₈
Quebec	9	3	0	0	149⁴/₈
Saskatchewan	81	43	17	3	171⁶/₈

Mexico Pope & Young Typical Entries				
All-Time Entries	**Last 5 Years Entries**	**Score 150 Up**	**Score 170 Up**	**Best Buck**
12	8	0	0	145⁶/₈

Southeast Pope & Young Non-Typical Entries

	All-Time Entries	Last 5 Years Entries	Score 170 Up	Score 190 Up	Best Buck
Alabama	4	2	2	1	$197^1/_8$
Arkansas	13	1	8	0	$186^0/_8$
Florida	0	0	0	0	0
Georgia	9	4	3	0	$185^7/_8$
Louisiana	1	1	1	0	$174^0/_8$
Mississippi	3	2	2	1	$204^0/_8$
North Carolina	7	3	1	0	$181^0/_8$
South Carolina	0	0	0	0	0
Tennessee	5	1	2	0	$176^6/_8$

Northeast Pope & Young Non-Typical Entries

	All-Time Entries	Last 5 Years Entries	Score 170 Up	Score 190 Up	Best Buck
Connecticut	5	3	4	1	$231^7/_8$
Delaware	0	0	0	0	0
Maine	2	1	1	0	$170^2/_8$
Maryland	23	12	12	4	$195^1/_8$
Massachusetts	1	0	0	0	$150^5/_8$
New Hampshire	2	2	2	1	$208^2/_8$
New Jersey	6	2	2	1	$203^3/_8$
New York	26	15	8	2	$205^1/_8$
Pennsylvania	18	7	9	4	$203^3/_8$
Rhode Island	1	1	0	0	$156^6/_8$
Vermont	0	0	0	0	0
Virginia	7	4	4	2	$194^2/_8$
West Virginia	8	2	5	0	$189^1/_8$

Midwest Pope & Young Non-Typical Entries

	All-Time Entries	Last 5 Years Entries	Score 170 Up	Score 190 Up	Best Buck
Illinois	298	127	98	74	$251^6/_8$
Indiana	46	16	26	15	$221^0/_8$
Iowa	202	92	130	54	$240^4/_8$
Kentucky	35	12	20	7	$234^1/_8$
Michigan	43	15	20	10	$219^6/_8$
Minnesota	107	20	69	20	$224^3/_8$
Missouri	57	29	36	9	$269^7/_8$
Ohio	109	35	70	17	$238^6/_8$
Wisconsin	223	98	114	26	$231^5/_8$

Southwest Pope & Young Non-Typical Entries

	All-Time Entries	Last 5 Years Entries	Score 170 Up	Score 190 Up	Best Buck
Arizona	0	0	0	0	0
California	0	0	0	0	0
Colorado	13	5	7	2	$229^7/_8$
Kansas	164	60	113	54	$262^7/_8$
Nevada	0	0	0	0	0
New Mexico	0	0	0	0	0

If you want a Pope & Young buck you can't beat hunting in the Midwestern states.

In some regions of the Northwest whitetails really hit the alfalfa fields hard. Figure out the strategic funnels deer in the territory use and you could find yourself face to face with a giant whitetail.

Southwest Pope & Young (cont.)

Oklahoma	23	6	12	2	232^4/$_8$
Texas	38	20	16	4	225^7/$_8$
Utah	0	0	0	0	0

Northwest Pope & Young Non-Typical Entries

	All-Time Entries	Last 5 Years Entries	Score 170 Up	Score 190 Up	Best Buck
Idaho	2	0	1	1	197^7/$_8$
Montana	13	3	6	3	210^7/$_8$
Nebraska	40	15	21	9	279^7/$_8$
North Dakota	11	2	6	0	188^1/$_8$
Oregon	2	0	2	1	203^7/$_8$
South Dakota	20	6	12	3	202^2/$_8$
Washington	6	1	3	1	224^3/$_8$
Wyoming	1	0	0	0	162^6/$_8$

Note! 21 of the current state record non-typical bucks were harvested by hunters during the past 10 years, 8 within the past 2 years.

Canada Pope & Young Non-Typical Entries

	All-Time Entries	Last 5 Years Entries	Score 170 Up	Score 190 Up	Best Buck
Alberta	24	9	12	5	241^2/$_8$
British Columbia	1	0	1	0	181^5/$_8$
Manitoba	8	2	6	2	234^2/$_8$
New Brunswick	0	0	0	0	0
Nova Scotia	0	0	0	0	0
Ontario	3	1	2	2	197^3/$_8$
Quebec	0	0	0	0	0
Saskatchewan	3	1	0	0	165^5/$_8$

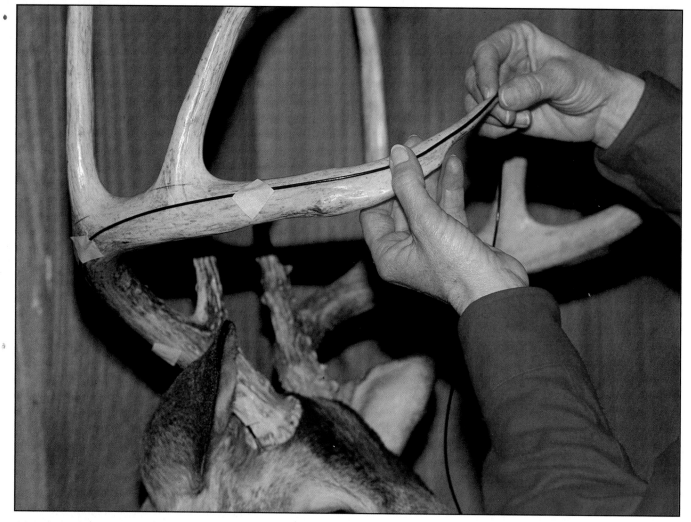

Main beam lengths contribute considerably to the score of a whitetail deer. Some whitetail main beams have reached almost 3 feet in length!

Mexico Pope & Young Non-Typical Entries				
All-Time Entries	Last 5 Years Entries	Score 170 Up	Score 190 Up	Best Buck
Mexico 0	0	0	0	0

TOP 10 STATES FOR BOONE & CROCKETT BUCKS

1. Iowa.
2. Illinois.
3. Wisconsin.
4. Kentucky.
5. Ohio.

6. Missouri.
7. Kansas.
8. Minnesota.
9. Texas.
10. Indiana.

The number of high-scoring deer from the Southeast is increasing, primarily because of quality deer management. Both individuals and state agencies are involved in this trend.

The author noticed this rack sticking out of a trash bag in a small building used by a taxidermist at an Illinois deer check station. Killed by Mike Ellis, the deer cranked out a score of 191-6/8 inches and is currently one of the top 10 typical bucks ever tagged in Illinois.

SCORING YOUR OWN TROPHY

The Boone & Crockett Club has an online scoring calculator that will enable you to score your own trophy animal. Simply log on to the Internet and type in www.boone-crockett.org. Once their home page appears, click on "Scoring Calculators." When the next screen appears, click on the species and type of animal you are scoring, such as Typical Whitetail Deer, and the proper scoring chart will appear. It then is a simple matter to score your own animal. You can even print out the score sheet when you're done.

Keep in mind this is an unofficial score. For the nearest official scorer in your area you can call the Boone & Crockett Club at 406-542-1888, or e-mail them at cdt@boone-crockett.org.

For Pope & Young scorers, simply access the Internet and type in www.pope-young.org. When their home page appears, click on "Measurer Information," then "Find A Measurer" and you will be able to access the name and phone numbers of all official Pope & Young scorers.

Both the Boone & Crockett Club and the Pope & Young Club are outstanding conservation organizations that contribute considerable money to preserve both our environment and our hunting privileges. Much valuable information about the work they do is listed on both of their Web sites. Also found there are many frequently asked questions about joining their organizations and about the scoring process.

Boone & Crockett's Top 10 Typicals

Rank	Score	Year	Location	Hunter
1	$213^5/_8$	1993	Saskatchewan	Milo Hanson
2	$206^1/_8$	1914	Wisconsin	James Jordan
3	$205^0/_8$	1971	Missouri	Larry W. Gibson
4	$204^4/_8$	1965	Illinois	Mel Johnson
5	$204^2/_8$	1967	Alberta	Stephen Jansen
6	$202^6/_8$	1992	Saskatchewan	Bruce Ewen
7	$202^0/_8$	1918	Minnesota	John A. Breen
8	$201^4/_8$	1974	Iowa	Wayne A. Bills
9	201	1961	Minnesota	Wayne G. Stewart
10 (tie)	$200^2/_8$	1983	Saskatchewan	Peter J. Swistun
10 (tie)	$200^2/_8$	1993	Illinois	Brian S. Damery

In 2000 Robert W. Smith took a gigantic typical in Pendleton County, Kentucky. If its unofficial score of $204^2/_8$ inches holds up when panel measured, it will tie as the fifth best typical ever taken in history.

Boone & Crockett's Top 10 Non-Typicals

Rank	Score	Year	Locality	Hunter
1	$333^7/_8$	1981	Missouri	Picked up
2	$328^2/_8$	1940	Ohio	Picked up
3	$295^6/_8$	1995	Mississippi	Tony Fulton
4	$284^3/_8$	1892	Texas	Unknown
5	$282^0/_8$	1973	Iowa	Larry Raveling
6	$281^6/_8$	1994	Louisiana	James H. McMurray
7	$280^4/_8$	1987	Kansas	Joseph H. Waters
8	$279^6/_8$	1991	Alberta	Neil J. Morin
9	$277^5/_8$	1976	Alberta	Doug Klinger
10	$277^3/_8$	1962	Nebraska	Del Austin

Awaiting to be panel measured for Boone & Crockett's top 10 non-typical category is a huge buck taken by Jerry D. Bryant in Fulton County, Illinois in November of 2001. Its unofficial score at this time is $291^1/_8$ inches!

Southeast Boone & Crockett Entries			
	Typical	**Best Buck**	**Non-Typical**	**Best Buck**
Alabama	11	$186^3/_8$	10	$259^7/_8$
Arkansas	73	$189^0/_8$	37	$238^3/_8$
Florida	0	0	2	$201^3/_8$
Georgia	113	$191^4/_8$	30	$240^3/_8$
Louisiana	36	$184^6/_8$	19	$281^6/_8$
Mississippi	36	$182^7/_8$	23	$295^6/_8$
N. Carolina	12	$181^7/_8$	3	$228^4/_8$
S. Carolina	4	$176^0/_8$	2	$208^5/_8$
Tennessee	20	$186^1/_8$	10	$244^3/_8$

Northeast Boone & Crockett Entries			
	Typical	**Best Buck**	**Non-Typical**	**Best Buck**
Connecticut	4	$179^4/_8$	5	$231^7/_8$
Delaware	9	$185^4/_8$	2	$190^4/_8$
Maine	76	$193^2/_8$	36	$259^0/_8$
Maryland	87	$185^7/_8$	17	$228^4/_8$
Massachusetts	4	$177^5/_8$	1	$188^2/_8$
New Hampshire	29	$183^3/_8$	6	$211^4/_8$
New Jersey	2	$189^4/_8$	2	$203^3/_8$
New York	43	$198^3/_8$	15	$244^2/_8$
Pennsylvania	21	$182^6/_8$	11	$213^6/_8$
Rhode Island	0	0	0	0
Vermont	3	$171^0/_8$	0	0
Virginia	54	$189^2/_8$	26	$257^4/_8$
West Virginia	11	$182^3/_8$	6	$231^5/_8$

Midwest Boone & Crockett Entries			
	Typical	**Best Buck**	**Non-Typical**	**Best Buck**
Illinois	348	$204^4/_8$	229	$267^3/_8$
Indiana	105	$195^1/_8$	54	$251^4/_8$
Iowa	401	$201^4/_8$	245	$282^0/_8$
Kentucky	200	$204^2/_8$ (pend.)	109	$243^3/_8$
Michigan	96	$198^0/_8$	65	$238^2/_8$
Minnesota	358	$202^0/_8$	264	$268^5/_8$
Missouri	204	$205^0/_8$	94	$333^7/_8$
Ohio	163	$191^5/_8$	92	$328^2/_8$
Wisconsin	438	$206^1/_8$	202	$247^3/_8$

Southwest Boone & Crockett Entries			
	Typical	**Best Buck**	**Non-Typical**	**Best Buck**
Arizona	0	0	0	0
California	0	0	0	0
Colorado	18	$186^3/_8$	13	$258^2/_8$
Kansas	166	$198^2/_8$	113	$280^4/_8$
Nevada	0	0	0	0
New Mexico	0	0	0	0
Oklahoma	43	$185^6/_8$	48	$247^2/_8$
Texas	224	$196^4/_8$	118	$284^3/_8$
Utah	0	0	1	$209^5/_8$

While some bucks don't make the official Boone & Crockett record book, they make the character record buck.

Northwest Boone & Crockett Entries			
	Typical	**Best Buck**	**Non-Typical**	**Best Buck**
Idaho	26	$182^5/_8$	31	$268^0/_8$
Montana	70	$199^3/_8$	45	$252^1/_8$
Nebraska	96	$199^2/_8$	50	$277^3/_8$
North Dakota	30	$194^7/_8$	17	$254^6/_8$
Oregon	7	$178^2/_8$	0	0
South Dakota	61	$193^0/_8$	36	$256^1/_8$
Washington	19	$181^7/_8$	31	$244^4/_8$
Wyoming	11	$191^5/_8$	21	$261^5/_8$

Canada Boone & Crockett Entries			
	Typical	**Best Buck**	**Non-Typical**	**Best Buck**
Alberta	186	$204^2/_8$	106	$279^6/_8$
British Columbia 20	$185^4/_8$	18	$245^7/_8$	
Manitoba	73	$197^7/_8$	32	$263^6/_8$
New Brunswick	28	$182^7/_8$	13	$249^7/_8$
Nova Scotia	6	$193^6/_8$	12	$273^6/_8$
Ontario	25	$177^7/_8$	8	$250^1/_8$
Quebec	3	$173^0/_8$	1	$198^4/_8$
Saskatchewan	290	$213^5/_8$	144	$265^3/_8$

Mexico Boone & Crockett Entries			
Typical	**Best Buck**	**Non-Typical**	**Best Buck**
27	$184^5/_8$	6	$223^6/_8$

Chapter 14

Dot-com
Deer
Hunting

Numerous map-related programs and journals are available for use on your personal computer.

DeLORME
Topo USA

MAPTECH®

Terrain Navigator

INDIANA
Southern
Evansville
New Albany

USGS topographic maps on CD-ROM, with powerful navigation software

Scroll seamlessly from map to map, or view individual maps, complete with collars

For hikers, bikers, hunters, or anyone planning an outdoor trip

For professionals who need high-quality, topographic maps

Web: www.maptech.com

Deer
Hunter's
Journal

For Windows 95 & Higher

Just sit back and enjoy the huntin'.

Citizens of the United States sat with their eyes riveted to their TV sets during the 1991 Persian Gulf War with Iraq. With amazement they watched as American missiles traveled hundreds of miles, then, as cameras relayed the images to the world, they hit their targets with pinpoint accuracy, actually traveling into the doors of the elevator shafts housing Iraq's dreaded Scud missiles. Until then people believed accuracy such as this was virtually impossible.

A subject such as this may seem completely unrelated to deer hunting. But it isn't. Laser devices guided the missiles, and 16 Global Positioning System satellites provided precise, worldwide, three dimensional position, velocity and timing data.

Now think about how deer hunting has evolved in recent years. Many hunters use laser rangefinders, several of which are accurate to within 1 yard out to 1,000 yards. And handheld Global Positioning System (GPS) units are commonplace among the hunting community. You can use them to find your stand site, find your way back to your vehicle, locate hot fishing spots on large bodies of water,

and for various other navigational uses. With some highly sophisticated GPS units now on the market, you can determine your position on earth to within 2 or 3 feet!

Yes, hi-tech instruments just keep becoming more and more sophisticated. This chapter will be geared toward those of you who are computer owners and are hooked up to the Internet. I'll share with you the latest developments in electronic technology that will enable you to become an even better whitetail hunter than you already are.

Dot What?

Well over 50 percent of American families now have at least one wireless phone, a 33 percent growth in just the past two years. Internet growth is similar. By the time you read this, at least half of you, or more, will have a computer in your home that will be hooked up to the Internet. While this gives you access to a tremendous amount of information, the Internet will never replace the printed page. Instead, the two will go hand-in-hand, being informational and useful in their own ways. For instance, as you read this chapter you can hook up to

Topographical maps are available on CDs. Each CD contains many quadrangles. These CDs are a great bargain and will allow you to pick out deer terrain traps in a large portion of your state.

By using the www.mytopo.com Web site, you can order a custom topographical or aerial map centered directly over your favorite hunting site.

your Internet Service Provider and follow along as I explain how to use different Web sites with a wealth of information about topographical and aerial maps.

I'll discuss several Web sites, and each of them will contain excellent map-related information. On several of these sites you can actually view and print free copies of parts of topographical and aerial maps. I'll even share a few neat little tricks about these sites which will allow you to find strategic stand sites, and point out tools on the Web site that will tell you what wind direction you should use.

Getting In The Center Of Things

After you have hooked up to the Internet and typed in "www.mytopo.com" a screen will appear. Under **Start Building Your Map Or Photo** you can enter the map location you desire either by place name or by latitude and longitude. Enter this information and click on **Go**. A list of topographical maps of the general region will appear. Click on the one you desire and the map will appear on the screen. To move to the exact location you desire, use the pan arrows around the map. They will move the map in any direction.

In the center of your map you will notice a map boundary box. Click on this box, then let off, and you will be able to roll your mouse around and reposition this box. Once it is where you want it, click on the box again and it stops moving. This box is the key to the uniqueness of the web site since it allows you to center your hunting area on a topographical or aerial map. Once this area is centered, you can preview the map. If you desire, you can change the map scale from 1:30,000 Most Area, to 1:24,000 Traditional, or to 1:15,000 Most Detail. You also can click Wide or Tall to change the map shape you order. Once it's laid out precisely as you want it in the preview, you can save the map and give it a name. You can print this map out free of charge, or if you desire you can order a waterproof copy of the map. You can order waterproof aerial maps in the same manner.

I use these waterproof maps and they work great and are reasonably priced. They are especially useful if the region you are hunting is located where four different quadrangles come together. If you buy separate quadrangle maps, it will take four maps to cover this situation, while one custom map from mytopo.com will do the trick. This saves you money and the hassle of fitting the other four maps together.

This site works great for creating maps you can hold in your hand. But www.maptech.com goes one better in this electronic age.

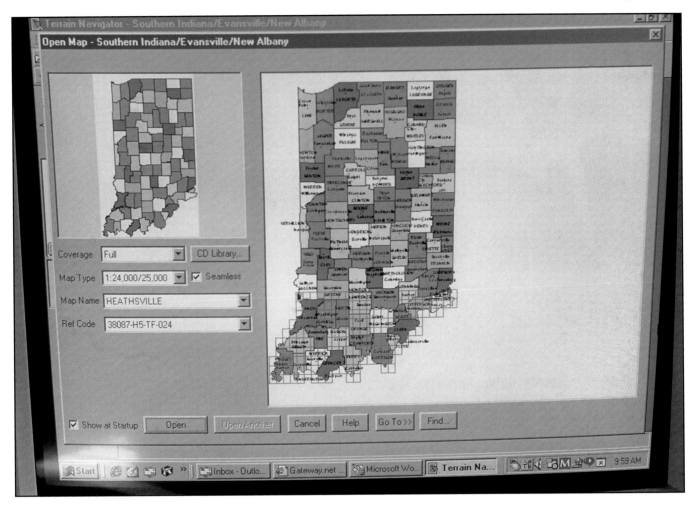

An Awesome Web Site For Maps

Type in "www.maptech.com" and you will enter one of my favorite sites for viewing topographical maps. Once there, click on **Online Maps, Charts & Photos**. On the drop down menu, click on **Start Mapserver.** On the next screen type in the city and state you are interested in and click **Go**. This search result will list all topographical maps available of this region. Then simply click on the topo map you want to view and it will appear on your computer screen. The detail is excellent, showing all elevation contours, roads, houses, ponds, streams, and many other terrain features of use to you as a deer hunter. You can move your view of this particular quadrangle map in any direction simply by using the triangular arrows found around the map's perimeter. Move the map around until it covers your exact area of interest. If you desire, you can print out a copy of the map at this time. This costs you nothing, and you can give copies to your friends who hunt with you.

Keep in mind while viewing this map that you can also zoom in and out to make the map bigger and smaller, and even switch over and get aerial views of

This Maptech CD of topographical map quadrangles covers approximately one fourth of the state of Indiana.

the same region in most parts of the country. Another neat thing you can do is e-mail the map to a friend. This works particularly well when you have three or four friends who hunt with you. You simply e-mail everyone a copy of the hot new deer hunting region you've uncovered, then everyone can study the terrain and offer their ideas on how it can best be hunted. You'll find the e-mailing information under **Fun Tools.**

Using Terrain Navigator

Now we get to the really neat part of this Web site; the Terrain Navigator. Click on this line and it will bring up information. If you want to wait on it, you can actually download a demo of the Terrain Navigator to see how it works. My advice, however, especially if you already use topographical maps, is to simply order the region of the state you hunt in from Maptech on one of their CD-ROMS.

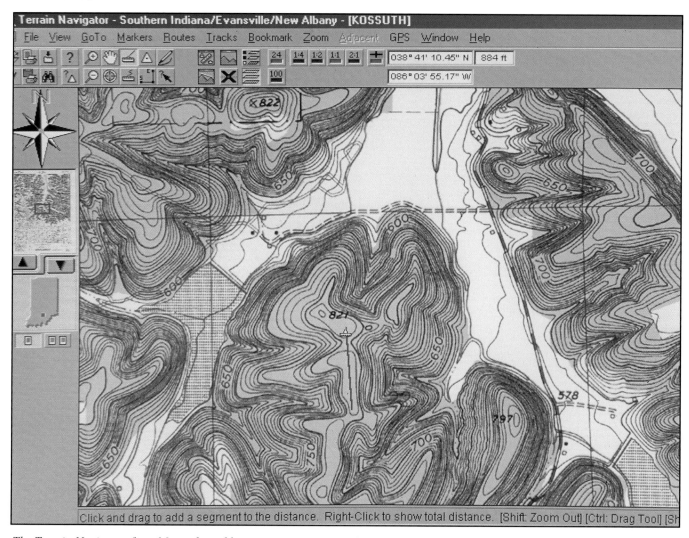

The Terrain Navigator from Maptech enables you to view topographical maps on your computer screen. Various tools with this program include distance rulers, and line-of-sight and elevation readings, among others.

This small CD contains 201 topographical map quadrangles.

It comes with the Terrain Navigator included and will include several 7.5-minute quadrangles. For example, the region I ordered was the southern portion of Indiana. It was $49.95 and included 201 quadrangles. If I had purchased these from the United States Geological Survey in printed form they would have cost me more than $800! Cost for all quadrangle maps in the entire state of Indiana is only $99.95.

Now I can install the Terrain Navigator, bring up the index map of Indiana and access any quadrangle in the southern part of my state. And, no, this isn't slow like the Internet. Since you're working off of a CD, the map appears instantly, and you can scroll across the map rapidly in any direction. You can hop over to the next quadrangle at warp speed, too. What this all means is that I can scan every quadrangle in southern Indiana and discover every terrain hot spot for deer there is. Then, I can either print any portion of a map I want to from the Maptech CD, or order the complete 7.5 minute printed quadrangle from the USGS, an online map

Can your computer and a map program help you figure out how to kill a wise old buck such as this? You bet they can!

company, or some other map dealer who partners with the USGS.

Amazing Terrain Navigator Tools

While I cannot explain everything the Terrain Navigator will do with a map, I'll give you as many details as I can. Trust me, this is one neat piece of electronic equipment. Let's assume the quadrangle you're interested in is a hilly region and you discover a strategic saddle way back in the hills, one you know big bucks will use when traveling about during the rut.

The next thing to do is determine your parking spot, and since it is a long haul in and out, you may want to know exactly how far you will have to walk. This is easily accomplished by using the **Distance Tool**. You simply click on the ruler, then click at the position where your

vehicle will be parked. Keep holding your mouse button down, and mark the way you would walk in. As you do this, at the bottom of the screen it will tell you exactly how far you have traveled as you mark your trail.

I also favor the distance tool using a straight line. In this case, we'll say we have found an awesome inside corner at the end of a large cornfield. Deer will use this heavily during daylight hours to avoid being seen, but we need to determine what wind direction to use so the deer won't pick us off.

In this case I use the straight line **Distance Tool**, and click on my exact tree stand position in the inside corner. Holding the mouse button down, I can swing this straight line in a full circle, giving a reading in degrees. As you know, a circle contains 360 degrees and we measure the degrees in it in a clockwise direction. Remember, too, that north is always at the top of a map. This means as I swing the distance tool, if it says 90 degrees, this means the line is running directly east of my tree stand. If it says 180 degrees, I'm south of my stand. 270 degrees would be directly west, and so forth. Doing this enables me to

The National Weather Service Web site gives you an up to date report about the weather. This includes hazardous weather warnings, long term forecasts and wind directions for your specific part of the nation.

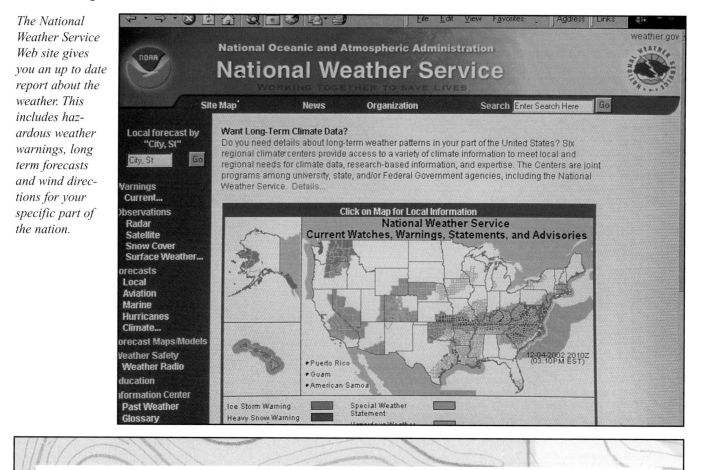

Some sporting goods stores, National Forest offices, and other places may carry topographical maps. For best results, though, and 100 percent order fill, contact USGS Information Services, Box 25286, Denver, CO 80225, phone 888-275-8747, fax 303-202-4693. Their Web site is www.usgs.gov. On their Web site, click on Online Maps and Photos, which will be found under Explore Our Products and Data. This will in turn take you to View USGS Maps and Aerial Photo Images Online.

Once to this location you will find listed several links such as www.terraserver.com, www.mapmart.com, www.maptech.com, www.topozone.com and www.terrafly.com. For a complete list of companies carrying the USGS products, simply click on Business Partner Program and it will give you this information.

There are several great map links on the Internet, with outstanding map products and information. For example, on www.terrafly.com, you can pull up one of their aerial photographs and click on a spot you're interested in and it will give you detailed information about this particular location. This information includes the population of the state, the population of the nearest town, the name of the county, the Congressional District, and even the name of the township. The name of the township, incidentally, will help you find landowners in this region that are listed in plat books.

For those of you new to topographical maps, www.topozone.com lists a Topo Maps Symbols page that will give you all of the information regarding symbols on topographical maps. This includes all water, land, road, and building symbols. This will be immensely useful for you first-time topo map users.

For a more comprehensive list of Web sites containing information about topographical and aerial maps, simply type topographical map or aerial map into a search engine and a list of numerous Web sites will appear. Some of my other favorite Web sites for topo and aerial map information are www.mytopo.com, www.maptech.com, www.mapmart.com, www.terraserver.com and www.delorme.com. You will most likely find several of your own favorite Web sites that may be different than mine. Check them all out as time permits.

Regarding information in this chapter, keep in mind that the information found on the Internet is changing constantly, and many Web sites are frequently redesigned. I have listed, and checked, the information contained in this chapter for accuracy right up until the last possible time before publication. Things sometimes change. So if you don't find what you want, just keep looking.

Maptech's Terrain Navigator contains information listing the meaning of all symbols found on a topographical map.

determine what wind directions I could best employ to keep my scent from blowing into the whitetail's line of travel. In truth, this straight line shows me precisely where my scent will be carried with every wind direction. Actually, when we lay a compass on a printed topographical map to determine what different wind directions might do, we're doing the same thing, only it's much more difficult since we have to position the top of the map directly north so it will match the compass direction.

Other Unique Tools

As you move your cursor around on your map, the Terrain Navigator continually tells you, at the top right of the screen, the longitude and latitude, as well as the changes in elevation. You can run an elevation profile using this, getting an idea of how steep a hillside is sloped. And by the way, information can also be downloaded between this program and a GPS unit.

Another really handy item is the Adjacent quadrangle feature. To use this, click the **Two Map** icon at the bottom left of the screen, then hit **Adjacent** in the tool bar and click on a topo map listed there. The screen will then show two adjacent maps at the same time, with all contour lines matching perfectly.

There is also a 3-D feature giving you the option of viewing two images side-by-side; one in 3-D and the other as a flat map. Or if you wish, you can view the entire map in 3-D from any angle. Seeing in 3-D will help many deer hunters to better visualize what the terrain looks like.

The information I have just shared should give all of you deer hunters out there something intriguing to research during the cold winter months. I fully realize those of you without a computer and an Internet hookup probably haven't understood much of this. But that will change. Years ago many people said they would never hook up to electricity, or a sewer system, or ever get a phone. Yet everyone did. So it will be with the Internet.

All of this electronic information I have just listed is truly fascinating and you can spend many enjoyable hours studying the geographic details it provides. In the end, though, it is the time afield that will bring all this deer hunting information together for us to use.

References

References
Map companies:

DeLorme
Two DeLorme Drive
P. O. Box 298
Yarmouth, Maine 04096
Phone 800-511-2459
www.delorme.com

Intrasearch, Inc.
12424 East Weaver Place, Suite 100
Englewood, Colorado 80111
Phone 303-759-5050
www.mapmart.com

Maptech
10 Industrial Way
Amesbury, Massachusetts 01913
Phone 888-839-5551 or 978-792-1000
www.maptech.com

myTopo.com
P. O. Box 2075
One South Broadway
Red Lodge, Montana 59068
Phone 406-446-1007
www.mytopo.com

High Performance Database Research Center
at Florida International University
11200 SW 8th Street, ECS243
Miami, Florida 33199
Phone 305-348-1706
www.terrafly.com

Maps a la carte, Inc
73 Princeton Street, Suite 305
North Chelmsford, Massachusetts 01863
Phone 978-251-4242
www.topozone.com.

USGS Information Services
Box 25286
Denver, Colorado 80225

Phone 888-275-8747
www.usgs.gov

Organizations
Boone & Crockett Club
250 Station Drive
Missoula, Montana 59801
Phone 406-542-1888
www.boone-crockett.org

Pope & Young Club
P. O. Box 548
Chatfield, Minnesota 55923
Phone 507-867-4144
www.pope-young.org

Weather
US Dept. of Commerce
National Oceanic and Atmospheric Administration
National Weather Service
1325 East West Highway
Silver Spring, Maryland 20910
www.nws.noaa.gov

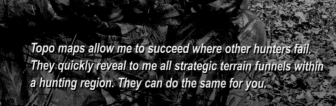